Behind the Stable Door

Behind the Stable Door

Horse and Pony Care

Brian Giles
Cartoons by Jake Tebbit

Stanley Paul
London Melbourne Sydney Auckland Johannesburg

Stanley Paul & Co. Ltd

An imprint of the Hutchinson Publishing Group

17–21 Conway Street, London W1P 6JD

Hutchinson Group (Australia) Pty Ltd
30–32 Cremorne Street, Richmond South, Victoria 3121
PO Box 151, Broadway, New South Wales 2007

Hutchinson Group (NZ) Ltd
32–34 View Road, PO Box 40–086, Glenfield, Auckland 10

Hutchinson Group (SA) Pty Ltd
PO Box 337, Bergvlei 2012, South Africa

First published 1983
© Brian Giles 1983
Cartoons © Stanley Paul & Co. Ltd 1983

Set in Baskerville by
A-Line Services, Saffron Walden, Essex

Printed in Great Britain by The Anchor Press Ltd and
bound by Wm Brendon & Son Ltd, both of Tiptree, Essex

British Library Cataloguing in Publication Data
Giles, Brian
Behind the stable door.
1. Ponies – Juvenile literature
I. Title
636.1'6   SF315

ISBN 0 09 151601 3

To Shirley, Sarah and Pippa
without whose help and encouragement
this book would not have been possible

Contents

About the author

Brian Giles has ridden horses and ponies since he could walk and cannot remember a time when they did not play a major part in his life. After being taught to ride properly by former point-to-point rider Yvonne Knowles, he finally left school and home to become an apprenticed jockey to the Queen Mother's trainer, the late Major Peter Cazalet. After several happy years spent at Fairlawne, near Tonbridge, in Kent, he left racing to take up a career in journalism and is now Equestrian Correspondent of the *Daily Mail*. He has travelled the world writing about horses and is one of the few journalists to have been invited to the home of Princess Anne and Captain Mark Phillips at Gatcombe Park.

His other books include *Twenty-Five Years in Show Jumping*, written with David Broome, and *Show Jumper*.

Acknowledgements

My thanks to Jake Tebbit for his excellent cartoons, my long-time friend Allan Parker for the instructional pictures, Pamela Crosher for the typing of the manuscript and to Marion Paull who edited the book for me.

1
Your first pony

Buying a first pony is as important to a young person as learning the green cross code. Make one mistake and the result could be disastrous, not only for the person who is doing the buying but for the pony as well. Too many people, parents included, think that being an owner is a status symbol – it is not, and anyone who holds such views should not buy a pony.

It is an awesome responsibility because although a pony can bring great joy and happiness to all concerned, it must be understood that equestrian activities can prove extremely expensive and, once bought, you will have complete charge of and responsibility for a living creature. That is not to be undertaken lightly.

I have seen too many mistakes to be lenient on this and even at the risk of being considered over-cautious, I want everyone to understand the points I have made.

Having written an equestrian column in the *Daily Mail* for ten years, I have been asked thousands of questions about horses and ponies by a cross-section of the public. After studying those questions and being told about many unhappy experiences, I can say quite definitely that a lot of the mistakes could have been avoided had the people concerned known how to deal with horses and ponies.

Several years ago, one youngster sent me a letter saying, 'My Dad bought me a pony, I feed him on bread all the time but he still seems to be hungry.' And although many people would condemn her out of hand, that child did at least have

He must have a home of his own

the good sense to ask 'Why?' and that is very important. The point I am making is that buying a pony means that you must first learn how to take care of it properly, and you can only do that by asking questions all the time, reading extensively and gaining practical experience.

Buying your first pony is a family affair and although your parents are going to be spending the money, they must also be made well aware that you will probably be needing more than their financial help. There will be times when you will have to rely on someone else attending to your pony's needs because you cannot be there due to ill health, schooling, or some other reason. And, if your parents are not too well up on the subject, it can prove to be a problem. In such cases, you will need a friend who is 'horsey' and who can be relied upon to help out.

Before you even look for a pony you should decide whether

or not you are going to keep him at home, in which case there must be a stable or field available, preferably both, in which he can live. If you do not own, or are unable to rent, such facilities, the pony will have to be kept at livery. This means that you will pay someone else to keep him at their stables. The cost will depend upon whether the pony is at grass or stabled and upon how much work – mucking out, grooming, exercising and so on – you are able to do yourself and how much you will expect the livery stable owners to do for you. Many riding schools take liveries and if he is going to stay at the local riding school, arrange to meet the owner beforehand and make certain he or she is able to accommodate an extra mount and that you can afford the charge that will be made, whatever it is. It will definitely not include shoeing bills and veterinary expenses but could well incorporate VAT and hay surcharges. It all accumulates very quickly.

Once this has been done you are ready to embark on a

Make sure he is the right size.

journey that will eventually lead to you becoming a pony owner. I say eventually because it might take anything up to three months, or even more, to find a suitable pony. It is a job which cannot be rushed and you must expect many disappointments before finally choosing the pony which is just right for you. Do not rush in and buy the first animal which becomes available because, although it could be the one for you, the chances are that it will not be. The mathematical odds against it are enormous.

Firstly, the pony must be the right size and shape. Buying one too big is just as ridiculous as buying one that stands knee-high to a grasshopper when you weigh 9 stone and are very tall. People, like ponies, come in all shapes and sizes and it would be silly for me, or anyone else for that matter, to recommend you to buy a pony of a certain height without knowing exactly what you weigh and how big you are.

Go to your local riding school, or District Commissioner of the British Horse Society Pony Club's local branch and ask for advice. They will at least be able to give you the size. Then it is a question of you making the right choice by looking at and trying as many ponies as possible.

Do not advertise in newspapers or magazines – you need to save all the money you can – but look instead in the equestrian magazines for those which are being advertised. *Horse and Hound*, a highly reputable publication, has columns of horses and ponies for sale each week and the chances are you will find something suitable there.

When you think you have found the pony you want, phone to make an appointment to see it, but do not go alone. It is most certainly a must to take with you an adult who knows about horses and who is prepared, if he or she is light enough, to ride the pony, negotiate with the owner and perhaps knock down the asking price. They will also know what points (good and bad) to look for, which you, as a novice, would probably miss. Tell the person who is selling the pony that you want to test the animal to the full and that, even if you like him, you will want him on trial and will need your vet (not theirs) to give him a thorough examination to see that he is healthy, and to confirm his age and height.

They might not like the idea, but that is their problem, and if they have nothing to hide and consider you trustworthy, there is no reason why you cannot come to a sensible agreement.

What you must remember is that your first pony must be safe, sound, have no vices and be positively traffic proof. Once it has been ascertained that he is safe in his box ask your companion to pick up his feet and touch his head and watch the pony's reaction. He should not lay his ears back, or try to nip you at any time. When his feet have been picked up check that the frog and sole on each one looks clean and healthy and that the hoof itself is not overgrown, cracked or ridged. Then watch while the saddle and bridle are being put on to see if there is any reaction from the animal.

He should not mind the bit going into his mouth and when the girth is being done up, he should stand still and not turn round to try and bite. Once this has been done ask for the pony to be led from the box to see how he goes through the door. He should walk sensibly through it and not dash out as though being chased by a thousand demons. Once he is in the yard ask for him to be led around so that you can see his action at a walk and a trot: both should be even and steady. Watch him all the time while he is moving.

Then ask the child who owns the pony to get on his back and ride him around a field so that you can see him put through his paces at walk, trot, canter and possibly gallop. This will tell you if he is responsive, i.e. if he goes forward, stops, etc. when asked to do so and does not buck or pull too hard, or dash sideways like a demented crab, or continually shy as though he has seen a ghost (if, indeed, there are such phenomena), while being asked to respond to the rider.

Having witnessed what everyone concerned will be hoping is a practical and worthwhile demonstration of his ability, you will have been able to get an idea of whether the pony is likely to be suitable for you to ride. If he is, put on the correct headwear (riding hat) and take him around the field yourself and do not show off. Just ask him to do all the things you would want him to do if you owned him, and start by seeing if he walks away from the field gate without hesitation.

If the field is average size, walk him once around it, then trot and canter on a figure of eight to test his balance and let your companion check that he leads off with the correct leg.

All the while he should be willing, and giving you a comfortable ride and he should not be making any gurgling noises while being exercised. If he is, then there is something wrong with his wind which your companion should also hear and start asking questions about.

If you are satisfied with the normal everyday movements, ask the owner to jump him for you over some small obstacles. At this stage of your career you will not be in training for a puissance and so will not be requiring him to leap great heights. You do need to know, however, what his capabilities are in case you wish to take him to a small show at a later date.

If that all goes well his next big test is to walk along a road where there is traffic passing. As this pony might be the first one you have ever owned in your life, he really must be 'bomb' proof. You simply cannot afford to have anything to do with one who hates the sight, or sound, of cars or tries to leap onto the kerb when a heavy lorry goes past, or one that dashes off at a mad gallop. The only way to prove that he is safe is for the person who usually rides him to take him out along the roads for you, while you watch their every move. If your companion is light enough to sit on his back let him or her put him to the test also.

Unless your tuition with your local riding school has taken you on roads at home and you know what you are doing, I suggest you do not ride a strange pony in traffic. Let the owner or the qualified person you take with you give a demonstration of his pony's merits, or bad points. With so many cars, lorries and such on the roads in Britain today, I advise you to stay well clear if it is at all possible. You and the pony might well be safe but it is those who are doing the driving who are the worry. Many have not got a clue about horses and that immediately puts you at risk, or at least at a major disadvantage.

Once you have made up your mind that you have found

the pony of your dreams you will need a written warranty of soundness and you should ask for a week's trial with the pony at your home or livery stable. It can prove expensive but in the long run it is worthwhile because if there are any hidden problems you might just find them then. Not all owners are willing to give trials, however. Remember that if you do take the animal away from his legal owner, before actually buying him, you would be well advised to have him insured for that period of time. Because, if you do not and something goes wrong, you might well find yourself in serious financial trouble and nobody wants that.

Make sure that proper arrangements with an insurance company have been made before travelling the pony back to your home. If you have no idea where the insurance companies are, the thing to do is to take a look in the yellow pages and ask your parents to phone for a quote. If the quotation is satisfactory, you could always insure the pony with a particular company when you have bought him. It does not cost a great deal and there are firms who, in fact, specialize in horse and pony insurance.

Apart from the cost of your pony, which could be anything from £200 to £800 or more (my first family pony was £250 and was a gem), you will also have to spend money to have your vet travel down (if you cannot have the pony on trial) to give the animal a thorough examination. Charges depend on where you live and can be ascertained beforehand by paying your local vet a visit, or phoning him.

But, believe me, it is money well spent. If you bought a pony without having a qualified person vet it, you could land yourself with hundreds of pounds worth of bills and a sick mount. Remember, once he has been bought the responsibility rests with you.

One man who fell into this trap said, 'I made the mistake of buying a pony without seeking advice from people who knew what they were doing because I thought I knew it all. But I soon found out I didn't. I bought my daughter a pony who was suffering from a foot disorder and we all had dreadful problems easing his pain and many veterinary bills to pay. If I had sought veterinary advice beforehand, I would probably not have bought the animal. After I did, it was up to me to look after him.'

That does not always happen, of course, but it does highlight the fact that you should seek expert advice before buying ponies or horses.

For someone who is lucky enough to have a sound one, the pleasures are enormous. It helps make them independent and gives them a sense of satisfaction which eventually develops into a healthy respect for all animals.

One other thing to remember is that before you buy any pony make sure that he can be caught in a field. It can be frustrating and time-wasting to spend hours trying to put a headcollar on him, when all he wants to do is gallop off like a wild horse.

Knowing the correct height of your pony is most important and it is information you will need if you ever want to sell him at some later date. A pony is always measured in hands and there are 4 inches to a hand, the measurement being taken from the ground to the point of the withers (the lowest point where the neck joins the spine). You will also have to know his height when you enter gymkhanas and small shows so that you can compete in the correct classes.

No matter how good you become, you will find there is nothing better than winning your first rosette. It is something you treasure, even if it was presented for finishing third in the 'family pony' competition when only four took part!

Although many people think that shows are for those who want to keep jumping ponies, that simply is not true and a lot of fun can be had from the small dressage events that are staged by the various branches of the Pony Club. Dressage competitions do not involve jumping and for the youngster who likes to think deeply about what is going on and believes he or she has a very intelligent pony, dressage events are ideal. Preliminary tests only involve carrying out normal everyday movements at given points in the arena.

They are also perfect for the youngster who, although he would dearly love to leap over fences, is rather nervous of jumping and would like to channel his riding talents in another direction. The great joy about dressage (a form of equestrian ballet – the first tests are a very elementary form) is that it can be practised on foot in the bedroom or lounge of your own home. All you need to do is acquire the test and then mark it out with paper on the floor. It is a wonderful way of learning the movements by heart, so that when you go to teach your pony, you, at least, know exactly what you are doing and can pass on the information to him.

It is a good sport to get you and your pony thinking and when performed properly is beautiful to experience and to watch. Another good thing about it is that at very junior levels if you cannot remember all the movements the judges will allow you to have a reader standing by the side of the arena who can shout out exactly what you and your pony should be doing at any given time. It is all good fun.

Dressage, like junior jumping, is a great leveller and to enjoy it to the full, you must learn to accept defeat with good grace, because you will be beaten far more times than you will win. The thing to remember is that with a first pony you are competing to take part, not to pot-hunt. It is a time of learning and if you start off on the right foot you will make lots of friends who will like you for what you are, not for how many prizes you win.

One young girl I know would ride in junior dressage competitions practically every week during the school holidays on her first pony who had, as it happened, a slightly stiff off-hind leg due to arthritis from old age. She knew only too well that no matter how hard she tried, her pony would probably never win because he simply was not physically capable of beating his rivals.

But they both persevered and won the respect of all who rode in dressage because they would enter competitions purely to take part and enjoy themselves. And that, you should always remember, is what sport or hobbies, at any level, are all about. By the law of averages, there must be more losers than winners, and if you make up your mind to be thankful and pleased that you are lucky enough to be a pony owner, and demand nothing else, you will have many happy years of riding.

The good and intelligent pony people are those who do not

make too many demands on their parents or their mounts, and who get just as much enjoyment out of talking and working with their mounts as others do galloping around all over the place.

Look after your pony properly and he will teach you more about himself and riding than you could ever imagine, which will stand you in good stead when you outgrow him and perhaps progress to horses.

2
The stable

If you are going to stable your pony, this chapter explains all you need to know. But it is by no means essential to have a stable for your pony. Most ponies of native breeding (Dartmoor, Exmoor, New Forest, Welsh etc.) will happily live out in a field right through the year providing a few rules are observed (see chapter 4 The Grass-Kept Pony). Instead of building their own stable, many people buy sectional ones to save time, hard work and a great deal of thought. And, in a world where time is precious, that is accepted. However, for those of you who want or need to build your own stable for personal satisfaction, or purely for economics (and a lot of people do), it is vital that you know exactly what it entails. You must also check with the local council to ascertain whether building permission is required before you begin.

Firstly, the siting of the stable is all important and must be fully understood. It really is astonishing how many people never even consider it when building a loose box for their horse or pony. The stable should face south so that when the cold northerly and easterly winds arrive, as they inevitably do, they are kept well at bay by the solid walls of the structure you have built. For a large horse, the measurements of the stable should be 4.3 metres by 3.6 metres with a height of 2.4 metres.

For a pony, think in terms of 3.6 metres by 3 metres. These sizes guarantee comfort and complete freedom of movement and that is exactly what you should be aiming to achieve. The point is that if you construct a loose box which is too small it could cause problems and it is far better to be on the generous side, then your horse will be comfortable and unlikely to knock or hurt himself.

There are several materials you can use to build the stable, including wood, brick and concrete and that choice must be left to each individual. You will certainly need a plan and because the box must be strong and competently put together, you will have to turn to a senior member of the family for assistance. He will supply most of the muscle (it is most certainly not light work and however keen you might be, you must also be practical) and will make sure that the building is as it should be. If the stable is being built of wood which has been put to use before, a careful search for any nails or bolts sticking out is essential. The dangers are obvious and if any are found they should be removed at once.

Before the base is laid, the floor foundation should be made up of rubble and then concrete poured on it to a depth of at least 33 centimetres. But it must have a slight slope for drainage purposes. The drain, when dug, is best placed outside the box for hygiene reasons, and you must also score the concrete before it sets so that it loses its smooth surface and is not slippery. Do remember though that the slope should only be enough for urine to flow down into the drain. If it is too steep the horse will be uncomfortable and may suffer leg strain.

The door of the stable should be in two halves so that the top section can be left open, allowing the animal to look out in winter and summer. This is extremely important because apart from keeping him healthy, it also gives him the opportunity of seeing what is going on and prevents him from becoming bored.

The door's size is also important. It must be high enough for your pony so that he does not bang his head going in or out, and it must be wide enough to allow him a clear passage. It must also open outwards so that if the horse gets cast behind it (that is if he lies down or rolls over with his feet or legs against the wall and cannot stand up again), you are still able to get to him. Failure to make the door the correct height and width could result in your pony being frightened

The stable floor shouldn't slope too much

and rushing headlong through it with you in tow. If it is not wide enough for him, it certainly will not let both of you through together and you could end up decorating the woodwork as your pony makes his charge. However, such unpleasant thoughts will never become reality if you stick to the right sizes.

There must also be a window in the box which hinges at the bottom and, ideally, is set above the head-height of the occupant. If, for some reason, that is not possible you must cover the glass with strong wire, or have metal bars put across to prevent the window being broken by the pony. Following this procedure, make sure the window can be easily opened, allowing plenty of light and ample ventilation, without draughts. This is essential, particularly during a hot summer, for the health of your horse. Stable waste can be fairly strong smelling at times and it would be wrong to leave the door and window shut, and not allow fresh air to circulate.

The loose box should also have lighting installed and this must be done by a qualified electrician because faulty connections could lead to fire, with disastrous results. The wiring must be insulated and placed where the animal cannot reach it with the switch outside the stable. You do not have to have a vivid imagination to realize what would happen if the horse or pony sank its teeth into the wire. The light bulb, like the window, must be convenient for you to reach, but out of mouth range of the animal and protected by wire mesh, which can be removed when the bulb needs changing.

The roof of your stable needs to be strong and rainproof and secured safely enough to withstand the strongest gale. If the building is not made of wood you would probably use slates or tiles, but hanging those correctly is an art and must be done properly to prevent one falling off and hitting you, or your pony, on the head. In no way are the problems insurmountable; it is just a case of what roofing materials to use. If you want to work with wood, remember that water-proof felt needs to accompany it and be firmly laid.

If, however, you cannot afford to buy everything you

require to build a new stable from scratch, it is perfectly all right to convert a shed or, indeed, any outbuilding, providing it really is suitable. It must be strong, safe, in no danger of crumbling to a heap on the floor, and large enough to accommodate your horse or pony. Such buildings are sure to be in need of repair and while you are doing that, and the conversion, the horse must not be living there. Supervision from an adult is essential because there is a lot of heavy work and some details on the plan you might find hard to understand. So don't be afraid to ask for adult help in order to get the work done and, who knows, they might even enjoy doing it.

Wanting and being able to afford to buy a sectional stable makes everything much easier because in many cases the cost of delivery and erection is included in the price. But each company does differ and it would be wise to check before making a firm order. Costs vary depending on the area in which you live, but to give you some idea a single unit, which has hardy timber framed walls and kickboards (to stop a horse kicking his way through the outer walls) would cost, at the time of writing, between £400 and £450. Each stable is fitted with guttering and drainpipes.

The good thing about this particular stabling is that you can buy as many units as you wish providing you have the money. In such cases, apart from laying the concrete base upon which the unit stands, you are involved in very little work.

If you think that this is the type of box you require, it is best for you or your parents to phone as many companies as possible and get the best quote. Many agents advertise in the equestrian press and a look through *Horse and Hound* and other specialist magazines, including *Riding*, *Horse and Pony* and *Pony*, will almost certainly reveal the advertising you seek. And, because everything is so expensive nowadays, once you have found what you are looking for do not be afraid to barter. This is an absolute must if you are intending to buy more than one unit – the money saved can always be put to good use at a later date. Keeping horses and ponies is an expensive pastime and there is no reason to think otherwise. So do not waste money, shop around, ask for discounts and if you do not get them with one agent go and find another. Do not take no for an answer – it is your money, so spend it wisely.

Some people, because of space problems, pressing financial reasons, or plain choice, keep their horses in stalls but others will not entertain the idea. They, like me, believe that a horse or pony needs ample room to move and, in general, feel comfortable through the day and night. Stalls do not afford them that opportunity with the same generosity since they are too narrow for the horse to turn round, and he must be kept tied up. Apart from any space consideration, some horses' lives can be made a misery particularly in swinging bail stalls if they happen to be alongside a misbehaved neighbour who kicks and bites and, in general, refuses to let the others around him rest.

A swinging bail stall is simply one which has a plank

Boredom leads to bad habits

hanging from the roof, suspended by strong rope, that divides one standing from the next. Normally this type of stabling is used by riding schools for horses who live out, and just need protection from the elements before going on their rides. The blacksmith might use them, too, to keep the horses he is shoeing in until it is their turn to have their feet attended.

For short periods they are fine but not for hours on end because, like you, horses and ponies get bored and you need to look after their minds as well as their bodies.

Boredom and unhappiness are the plague of the modern equine and should be prevented at all costs because they can so easily lead to trouble, particularly in the stable. Happy horses and ponies are wonderful creatures but abuse them by not troubling about them, or caring about their comfort and needs, and they can, with justification, be positively irritating. It should never be assumed that, because the animal's body is in good shape, everything else is also fine. The mental condition of your horse or pony is of the utmost importance otherwise he might start snapping at you when you enter the stable. Crib biting (getting hold of a projecting object with the teeth and sucking in air) and weaving, (moving the head from one side of the open top door to the other) are common habits which are extremely troublesome and should not be encouraged. They can also lead to other animals following your horse's lead. Prevention is better than cure and if you eliminate boredom you could have found the answer.

That is one reason why many people do not like 'corridor' stables, where the occupants live in boxes which are themselves housed within a building. Some racehorse trainers use this method and while it does block out a lot of sound and allows the horses to rest, I do not like it at all. Looking out, sometimes through prison like bars, at the half-tiled wall of a passage-way is not anyone's idea of a thrilling time and, perhaps, some horses feel that way, too.

The people who use this type of stabling do not mean any harm. Some might not even have given it a second thought, but perhaps they should. After all the loose box is the horse's home, not a prison and when you consider that the animal who lives in it spends an awful lot of time there, it is common sense to make it as comfortable and as interesting as we can. A comparison can be made with people who spend a long time in solitary confinement. After a while it becomes unbearable, even with exercise periods, and that is how it must be for a horse or pony at times. It is a point worth thinking about. This is why it is better, if you have a paddock as well as a stable, to turn your horse or pony out for an hour or two each day, particularly if he is not being worked very hard. He will enjoy the freedom and, provided he is protected from the weather in winter, he will come to no harm. If your pony has been clipped he must be turned out in a New Zealand rug.

Apart from the stable, you will also need somewhere to keep your pony's feed. Your feed store must be dry so that the contents are not ruined by damp and, eventually, mould. Although the feed bins (usually wood or metal containers) do not take up much space, the storage of hay and straw is a different matter. For these a fairly large outbuilding, with a good, solid rainproofed roof, would be ideal. But as such a building is not always available a shed, or even an area covered with tarpaulin, would suffice. The secret of storing hay and straw is to make certain that the floor space where it is going to be stacked is dry. If it is not, good hay will turn soggy, lose its quality and must not be used. Once you have made certain that the base is suitable the next move is to stack the hay properly, making sure that fresh air can circulate between the bales.

If you are lucky enough to have the storage space available, buying in bulk is always cheaper and, in the long run, a lot less work. Always remember, too, that good food is essential for a healthy pony, so never buy rubbish; it is a false economy. Hay should feel good and smell sweet and, if you are unable to buy in bulk, try and come to a sensible arrangement with a local riding school who always, of course, have large, regular deliveries. They know exactly what to order for their working horses and ponies and will be aware that there are three types of hay used for various purposes – meadow, mixture and clover. You will find that, of the three, meadow hay is cheaper and the most commonly used.

When you have stored the hay correctly it is always wise to shake it well before feeding it to the animals. This is a safety precaution to get rid of any dust which otherwise might affect the horse's lungs or digestive tract. It is all simply a question of thinking and being interested in what you are doing – which even stretches to haybale wire, or string. When you have cut it, pick it up and place it in an old sack for later use, or disposal. Never leave things lying about in or near a stable. For order and smooth running, a stableyard should be neat and tidy. That means that you are trying and your horse is being well looked after. Sloppy habits should not be tolerated under any circumstances.

There are many expensive gadgets you can buy for your stable nowadays, but those that just do the job for which they have been designed are usually the best. The manger, for example, can be made of strengthened polythene which is easy to clean but must be at a suitable height so that your horse does not have to perform miracles, or go through a series of gymnastics to reach his food.

At the back of the box you should fix a ring securely so that the pony's headcollar can be tied to it when necessary. This is put at the animal's chest level while another ring, for the haynet, should be placed at the height of his eyes. If the haynet is too high, dust and seeds could fall into his eyes. If it is too low there is a danger that the pony might catch his foot in it. I never like using too many metal objects in a stable and therefore recommend a rubber or plastic bucket in which to put water. Then, even if it gets knocked over or the horse picks it up with his teeth (and some do) and throws it across the stable, the chances of him being hurt are most unlikely.

Apart from the actual loose box and food store, you will need a tack room for your saddle, bridle, rugs and other equipment. Again, it does not have to be very large but it must be rainproof and have very strong locks attached to the door to dissuade thieves. Security is a major problem nowadays not only with houses but stables as well. Each year half-a-million homes are burgled, which is a dreadful state of affairs.

As far as the equestrian scene is concerned the police are investigating the thefts of thousands of pounds worth of tack from all over the country. Burglars abound in the horse world because stables and tack rooms are usually set well away from the house, which makes detection that much more difficult. And, because saddles and bridles are expensive to buy, there is a big market in second-hand goods and stolen equipment which can easily be sold on with few questions asked. The police, trying to catch the people concerned, have an unenviable job on their hands because trying to trace stolen tack is about as difficult as finding a reliable clue to the whereabouts of the Holy Grail.

What you can do to save yourself any unpleasantness and a great deal of money is to visit your local locksmith, tell him what you require to make the tack room safe, and ask him to recommend a suitable lock. If you can afford it, a burglar alarm system could be installed but that means a lot of money and only you and your family can decide whether it will be possible.

The actual stable should also be secure but, unlike the tack room, must not, under any circumstances, be locked while a horse or pony is inside. The reason for this is that if a fire broke out it must be possible to lead the animals to safety quickly. If you had locked the door, were not there at the time, and had the key in your pocket, the animals would be trapped. I am not writing this particular paragraph to frighten you, but merely to highlight the fact that you should not lock your horse's box.

Having said that, it is important that the stable door should have two bolts, the one at the bottom being foot operated, the top one designed with a clip catch. This simple, but highly effective invention, prevents the animal from pulling the bolt back with his lips, or teeth. There are some very clever and, indeed, naughty ponies about who are able to do this. Some of the tricks they perform would make even the cleverest magicians look like novices.

The bolt at the bottom helps strengthen the door if it gets a hefty wallop from a well-directed hoof, but both can easily be released from the outside.

It does not do always to look on the black side of things, but it is best to be prepared where animals are concerned. Never forget that fire is a very serious hazard. That is why you should have an extinguisher handy or if that is not possible, a large bucket of sand which will help put out flames. Nobody should be allowed to smoke in the stable area and if they insist, tell them nicely but firmly to be on their way. It is a risk you and your horses cannot afford to take.

Many of these safety aspects are really only common sense and, if people think about what they are doing, their horses will not come to any harm.

As an extra safety measure you should make frequent trips to your stable to check on your horse. If for some reason you cannot go yourself then send somebody you can trust. Being a horse owner is a 365-day a year pastime and if you are unable to devote that time it is advisable that you do not have your own horse or pony at home. If you can manage it, however, and work hard, then a whole new, exciting life will open up for you and your family.

3
Mucking out

Having decided upon the type of stable you want and having built it, or had it assembled, you will then become involved with its day-to-day running and the general care of your horse or pony. This is when everything really becomes fun. Even daily mucking out can be enjoyed if it is done properly.

First make sure you have the correct tools for the job: a pitchfork (two-pronged), an ordinary garden fork (four-pronged), a shovel, wheelbarrow, skep, mucksheet and a stiff-bristled, heavy-duty broom. It might sound a lot but once bought and, provided it is looked after, the equipment will last a long time and more than justify the initial cost.

Although you may not think all these tools are important, they are, and when finished with every day they should be cleaned and put away. Leaving them out in all weathers can lead to the wood of the forks rotting and the metal being weakened by rust. More importantly, if the tools are strewn about the yard, your horse could step on them and hurt himself. The thing to do is to make a permanent space for them in one corner of the room where you keep your tack. The wheelbarrow can easily be pushed out of the way under cover of a lean-to or shed. Then you know where everything is and can go straight to it the moment you want to start work in the stable.

If girls are doing the mucking out, I would suggest they wear gloves because it is so easy to acquire unwelcome blisters when shovelling, or forking solid bedding into a wheelbarrow and pushing it to the muck heap. These points are important if you want to keep reasonably clean hands and not have them covered in hard skin and infuriating little cuts in which dirt always seems to become ingrained. Boys never seem to mind what state their hands are in!

Mucking out is done daily because, like you, your horse or pony likes and indeed needs to sleep in a clean stable. Failure to do this can lead to the animal standing on soggy bedding which could cause him to develop thrush (a disease which attacks the cleft of the frog in the hoof). This is not pleasant for him and gives off a dreadful smell as the muck in the hoof rots. If mucking out is done properly and the feet are picked out regularly, at least twice a day, thrush will not be given a chance to gain a hold. It is only a lack of concern and cleanliness which allows it to start in the first place.

There are several types of bedding you can put down for your horse to sleep upon including straw, wood shavings and sawdust, peat moss and, a more recent innovation, shredded paper.

The straw you are likely to use would be either wheat, oat, or barley. Costs vary and can depend largely on whether the farmers have a good or a bad harvest. Some, alas, do find it cheaper to burn off the straw instead of gathering it. I am afraid it is a sign of the times and a period in our history when everyone is thinking of economy.

As a rule, horses are unlikely to eat wheat straw (although some greedy ponies will consume almost anything) while many will eat barley or oat straw, which should be discouraged. Straw has very little nutritional value and can also give the animal colic (abdominal pain). Also, barley, if it has not been combine harvested to rid it of the awnes (beards of barley) will cause scratches and irritation.

There are several methods of stopping horses eating bedding. One is to sprinkle a dilute solution of disinfectant over the straw, once it has been laid. Another, of which I disapprove, is putting a muzzle on the animal. If the pony is greedy it is preferable to bed him down on something which he is not going to eat, such as sawdust, shavings, peat or paper.

Every morning, armed to the teeth with fork, shovel,

broom and wheelbarrow and feeling remarkably like St George in search of a dragon, you will proceed to the mucking out. It is a job some people find tedious but one I thoroughly enjoy, because it is important and helps to keep me fit.

If you are unable to turn your pony out while changing his bedding, he should be tied up to the appropriate ring at the back of the stable to stop him getting in your way or walking out of the box while you are working. Also, always remember to remove the water bucket and haynet.

When this has been done remove the droppings and fork the wet and soiled straw or shovel wet sawdust etc. into the barrow, which has been placed just outside the door. After shaking the rest, pile it into one corner of the box. Afterwards sweep the floor as clean as possible and pick remaining droppings and wet straw up with the shovel and empty into the barrow. Then, using your fork, move the dry, used straw into another corner of the box and sweep clean where it had been standing.

While doing this you should be talking to the animal all the time to reassure him. When you want him to move from one side of the stable to the other just push him gently with your hands and make a clucking sound with your mouth.

Before mixing fresh straw with that which you have left in the box, let the stable floor have an airing, although if the pony cannot be exercised or turned out you must put a light covering of straw down so that he does not slip and slide all over the place.

When you are ready to remake the bed be sure to fork enough straw down for him to be comfortable and bank some of it up each side of the box. This will help prevent him becoming cast when he is trying to get up after lying down. Having emptied the manger of any remaining bits of food and thrown away the stale water, swish the bucket out and replace with fresh water. Also clean the manger well.

Compared with straw bedding, mucking out wood shavings and sawdust is, in my view, somewhat harder. Instead of using a fork, a shovel is more advantageous when removing wet bedding and droppings, but it is less kind to your muscles because everything is so much heavier. The prin-

Every horse likes to be comfortable

ciple is still the same and you must throw out any soiled bedding and rake over well what is left, adding new wood shavings and sawdust.

Many people have discovered that an ideal paper bedding is Diceabed (non-gloss) which has been cut by special machines. It is highly recommended because it is easy to handle and to store. Apart from these excellent qualities it is also available all the year round and is free from dust which, if you happen to own a pony who suffers from a respiratory problem, makes it a good bedding material.

It is also good for those doing the mucking out, particularly people like me who start wheezing at the drop of a straw bale because of the dust it contains. Anyone who has ever suffered from an allergy condition will know exactly what I mean.

You need between two and a half and three bales of Diceabed to set up your horse's box. It should be forked out onto the floor. The bed should of course be deep enough to make him comfortable.

A few years ago some old diehards might have scoffed at the thought of their prize hunters being stabled on paper, but this no longer holds good – certainly not if they want to be economical and practical.

When mucking out this particular bedding remove droppings and badly soiled paper, fork the rest up the sides of the wall and sweep the floor clean. While you are doing this, the semi-wet material will be drying. And, just for your notebook, paper dries very quickly, which is another advantage.

When the floor has been cleared replace the bedding on it evenly and then bank up the sides. With Diceabed you only need half to one bale a week to keep the bed clean and comfortable for your horse.

The old, waste paper has many advantages, too, and when finished with in the stable can be forked into the garden where it makes an excellent fertilizer. Tell your father he can grow mushrooms on it, among other things.

Allowing for the obvious fact that a dog is far smaller than a horse, the thing to remember is that the idea of bedding is the same. My wife bred a litter of puppies who spent all their early life sleeping on shredded paper, which proved to be ideal. Other great benefits from using it are that it really is hygienic, non-toxic, dust free and highly absorbent.

Apart from horses and puppies, the paper bedding is also used for cow cubicles, litter for poultry and bedding for pigs. At a time when money for practically everyone, particularly the young, is in short supply, paper appears to be a sensible, economic answer to some pony people's problems.

I mention this particular bedding and its prices in detail because I firmly believe that this is what most people will be using in the near future.

With every type of bedding, however, make sure you put enough clean back in at the end of the day. A thin covering overnight, which will enable parts of the pony's limbs or body to come into contact with the concrete floor can cause your pony to hurt himself or even develop capped hocks (bruising and subsequent swellings on the point of the hocks).

Apart from changing the bed and picking up droppings

with a skep regularly you should also disinfect the floor once a week to freshen everything and kill germs.

There is another method of bedding called the deep litter system where fresh straw, peat or wood shavings are put on top of existing bedding once the droppings and wet patches have been removed. The whole bed is only removed completely every three months or so and I do not like it at all. I need to know that my horse's box is clean, neat and tidy every day.

Another disadvantage of using deep litter is that when the entire bed is thrown out you may well need a lorry to take it all away and that is not always possible or practical. It can also create a lot of unnecessary expense.

This leads me to another important point. You must know how to transport soiled bedding to the muck heap – it is not just a question of pushing a barrow.

Sometimes, if it is full, the wheelbarrow can be very heavy and for some this can prove too exacting. The first thing to do is to hold the barrow's handles firmly then, bending your knees, lift the weight and ease it forward. Make two journeys instead of one and you will find it much easier and will not hurt yourself.

Trying to lift too much can cause you to strain stomach, or back muscles and that is to be avoided. Once you have a bad back it usually takes a long time to cure, as anyone who is a sufferer will confirm.

The muck heap, if designed properly, can be made to make waste products work for you, which is an important point. It should be sited someway from the house because although you might like the smell of horses, some other members of the family may not.

The muck heap should be contained within a three-sided brick wall, or corrugated iron framework, the back of which should be about 1.5 metres high, since soiled bedding is usually thrown as far back as possible. Keep the manure packed down tightly as this will help it to rot, which is exactly what you want.

Because you have to transport the manure to the muck heap every morning, you will want to make the exercise as

Make two journeys instead of one

easy as possible. This means putting down a suitable path so that the wheelbarrow will run easily along it and not wear you out in the process.

If you cannot afford to lay a proper path, go in search of rubble (old bricks and stones) and put that down. Ask a senior member of the family to help crush them into the ground. This will at least stop the barrow sliding in the mud and depositing its load everywhere.

After each mucking out session the area in front of the stable should be swept clean and any wisps of straw picked up and disposed of at once. Then all the tools should be cleaned thoroughly, including the wheelbarrow and skep which can be brushed out with the broom to prevent any muck sticking to the sides. Push the garden fork into earth several times, rub down the prongs with a piece of sacking and then, wearing a pair of old gloves to protect your fingers, pick out the strands of hay and straw from the bristles of the broom. After this has been done put all the tools away in a dry place ready to be used again at evening stables.

Getting rid of accumulated manure need not be a problem. Gardeners love to use it for vegetables and flowers and, in particular, roses. They are ready to buy bags of it from wherever they can and will also collect it. People who run allotments are always on the look out for manure fertilizer because of its growth-promoting qualities. The blacker the rotted manure the better as far as they are concerned and it is a great help to you if you do not have the bother of delivering it.

This, of course, is an excellent way of getting rid of manure and making you extra money in the process, which can always be saved to replace broken tools, or to buy more equipment.

4
The grass-kept pony

For the thousands of young people who own ponies and keep them at grass this chapter is probably the most important in the book and should be read, re-read and remembered. In a way, you will find that life is somewhat harder for you because your pony might be kept in a field some way from where you actually live, which will mean a twice daily journey to see him and check that all is well.

In fact, when the weather is really bad and the sleet and rain are hammering into your face like tiny needles, you may well be tempted to stay in the comfort of your own home and not bother to get a good soaking. You may even make up excuses for yourself and promise that whatever happens you *will* go and visit him the next day. It is so easy to do but if you allow it to happen you will be letting down your pony and yourself.

However, there are advantages to keeping a pony at grass. Firstly, it is more natural for him to be out of doors and eating grass and, secondly, he can exercise himself and therefore need not be ridden every day.

In times of doubt you must think deeply about what you are doing and tell yourself that you are among the privileged youngsters who can actually afford a pony, and as such you must also accept the responsibilities that go with it. Always remember that there are millions of people who will never be able to own any animal, let alone a pony, and to find yourself in such a very fortunate position is a time for thanks, not laziness or self-concern.

We will now get on to the actual business of keeping a pony at grass and all that it entails. To begin with, you will need a field or paddock of one acre per pony, whether it is at your home or nearby. For the moment we will assume that your parents own the land and you are able to make changes by just seeking their permission. The first thing to do is to check that the fencing around the field where you are keeping the pony is as secure as you can make it. Ideally, the area should be fenced in with solid posts and rails, with the uprights prominent on the far side of the fencing. The planks will be on the pony's side so that if he decides to gallop about he is not going to crash into any projecting pieces of wood.

There are other materials you can use to make a paddock or field safe, and if you cannot afford the expense of good post and rails, then wire strands will do, but you must have the fencing four strands high (the lowest being 1 foot from the ground) and the wire must be kept tight against the wooden uprights. The reason for this is that if the pony were to get himself caught up in the wire he could do himself

Never use barbed wire

irreparable damage. Never use barbed wire to fence off a field where horses and ponies are being kept, because the animals could tear themselves to shreds. Hedges provide good natural boundaries, as well as offering shelter, but they must be strong and preferably reinforced with fencing through the centre.

Apart from the actual fencing, the gate is also extremely important and should be kept shut with a latch in the middle and an up-and-over looped catch at the top. This makes it easy for you to open, but difficult for horses to do so, and is far smarter than having great lengths of string trailing all over the place.

If you do not own the field, then permission for any changes must be obtained from the person who does, but I cannot see anyone objecting to a field being made safe and secure.

If your pony or horse is being kept in a field which already has its own fencing, you must make sure that it is very strong, with no gaps or shaky uprights and no pieces of wood sticking out or nails protruding from the fencing. Checking all this out does not take very long and will, of course, make your pony safer than he might otherwise have been.

Horses and ponies do not mind cold, clear weather but when rain or sleet lashes down they start looking for somewhere they can shelter until it has passed. There is nothing worse than seeing a bedraggled pony in a field, soaking wet and with no protection. Even wild ponies and horses, who live out all the time, have some protection against the elements in the form of trees, bushes and even hills. Because he is in a fenced-off field, your pony or horse cannot go anywhere and so you must make sure that his requirements are catered for all the time.

It is always best to have a shelter in the field large enough for the animal to escape from really dreadful weather and, in the summer, from the wretched flies which can make his life a misery. The shelter should be completely open-fronted, facing south and preferably in a corner of the field or paddock. Being open-fronted, it will allow several ponies to pass each other safely in the entrance. It has, in fact, several purposes, because apart from being a permanent shelter from the weather that the pony can enter at will, it can also be used if the animal is unwell. In case of illness, it is necessary to have a proper method of blocking the front in. You would, of course, need to put down some bedding and supply fresh, clean water.

This also applies during a very severe winter, when the bedding will help to keep him warm.,

Do not for one moment think that all this is making too much unnecessary fuss, because it is not; all you are doing is affording him the proper protection that is due to him. Imagine how difficult it would be for you to cope if your pony became ill and you had no shelter for him.

When the post and rails, wire or hedge has been made secure, and you have erected a shelter, you must also make sure that there is an ample supply of fresh, clean water and if the field does not contain an old round-sided tub or, better still, a self-filling trough, you must bring water at least twice a day in two buckets. Tubs must be cleaned out and refilled weekly and checked daily. Self-filling troughs must also be cleaned regularly, but they are connected to the main water supply and refill themselves as soon as the horse drinks. I would not advise you to rely on a ditch in the field (which should be securely fenced off) even if it is usually full of water, as you cannot be sure where the water has come from. Never take chances – always make sure water is clean and fresh. In the winter you must also make sure that the water supply does not freeze. If it does, you must break the ice several times daily. If the water is coming from an outside tap, make sure that you cover the pipes well with some old sacking to stop them freezing up.

I must stress that the cleaning of the water container is very important because you will find that if you leave it, a green slime will stick to the inner rim and the pony will not want to drink from it at all. A simple test to prove the point is to fill an old jar up with water and leave it outside your house for a few days and see what state the container and water are in when you inspect it later.

In their natural habitat, horses and ponies will drink rain

water or fresh water from streams. With the riding horse or pony this is not always possible and so you must make sure that he has a constant supply of clean, fresh water.

While on the subject of water, make sure that the field in which you are keeping the pony or horse allows rain water to drain off, otherwise you will have pools of it lying about the place which will cause the field to churn up and will destroy the grass.

If you find that the drainage is bad, ask your parents to do something about it at once. If they do not know much about the land check with a local farmer or smallholder, who will probably be only too willing to give some useful advice. Even better, join the Young Farmers' Club in your area because then you will not only meet new friends, but also people who are interested in the land and its welfare. They are always useful people to know who will probably teach you a lot.

Anyone who is keeping a pony at grass should be well up on plants which are poisonous and in some cases cause death. It is not a pleasant subject to deal with, but one which must be studied in order to avoid any trouble. One of the most dangerous plants is ragwort, which is a yellow-headed weed common to pastureland. It is deadly and although some people just cut off the heads of ragwort, it *must* be removed completely from the field by the roots. The best thing is to dig up the whole plant, take it away from the horses and ponies and burn it to a cinder. Do not, under any circumstances, pull ragwort up and leave it lying about because, for some unknown reason, ponies who sometimes will not touch it while it is growing will certainly do so when it is not. Do not take any chances at all – pull it up and destroy it.

Plants from the hemlock family might well have been fine to help make the evil brew of witches but, as far as horses and ponies are concerned, they are completely taboo. They include deadly nightshade, water dropwort and cowbane. They all sound as though they could do you damage if you even mispronounced them! These plants should be removed in the same way as ragwort.

Add to that list the yew tree and acorns and you will be a

Poisonous plants stir up trouble

long way to knowing what to keep your ponies away from at all times. If you cannot get rid of the yew, ask whoever owns it to cut off the lower branches, take them away, and fence the whole thing off from the horses and ponies. Pick acorns up and throw them in a dustbin out of harm's way. I would also suggest you dig up any stinging nettles and thistles because they do not have any food value for the animals in your charge and are a waste of land, which could be used for grass.

If you have the pony in a paddock at home and your garden contains a privet hedge, do not, under any circumstances, allow anyone to feed your pony with the cuttings or let him eat the leaves. It is a poisonous hedge. Grass cuttings can also be dangerous – do not feed them under any circumstances.

If you are not sure how to identify poisonous plants, approach the District Commissioner of the local branch of the Pony Club or a Pony Club instructor and ask if she or he would be kind enough to drop by when passing and tell you. But whatever you do find out, be sure to take the appropriate action.

If Pony Club people are not available, approach one of the senior girls at the local riding school for advice. Anyone who has anything to do with horses knows how important it is not to let them eat the wrong things, and will normally be only too pleased to help. Once the poisonous plants have been pointed out, it is only a question of you getting rid of them.

Check your field for poisonous plants before putting the pony in it, and check regularly afterwards to ensure no more have sprung up. When pulling the plants up wear gloves or remember to wash your hands properly afterwards in a mild disinfectant. Even if you have a tree in the field or paddock which is not harmful to the ponies you will have to fence it off, because they may strip it of its bark and eventually kill it.

Keeping a pony, or ponies on a small acreage will most certainly lead to them having an acceptable level of worm infestation, which will give you a continuing battle to keep your pony in good condition. I mention a small acreage, in particular, because the ground on such land is more likely to keep on becoming reinfested with the wretched things.

They really can be a worry and if the paddock where you

keep your pony is small, then you must pick up the droppings so that the worm larvae do not reinfest the grass and, as a consequence, find their way back into the pony. There are several types of worms, the worst being the red worm which if left long enough can do untold damage to the animal's internal organs.

Have a regular worm count done on your mount because failure to cope with the worms will cause the pony to lose a lot of condition.

In order to have the worm count done, all you need do is take a sample of the animal's dung in a plastic container to your local vet, who will test it for you and tell you exactly what you need to know and how to cope with the situation. Always seek veterinary advice with a thing like this because it is so very important. The vet will work it all out and tell you exactly how often the animal needs to be fed a 'wormer'. His advice, believe me, is invaluable.

To help combat the worms and to keep the grass in your field healthy, you should practise rotational grazing, whereby parts of the paddock are fenced off and allowed to recover from grazing while the rest is being used. Failure to be sensible about this will result in your field becoming a fair imitation of the Sahara desert in summer and a Florida swamp in winter. Either way it will eventually become totally useless to your pony or horse and give you untold trouble.

You should also try to have the field harrowed and rolled and the appropriate organic fertilizers applied. The animal must not be allowed to graze in it for at least a month, until the fertilizer has been absorbed into the soil. Fertilizers can be harmful to horses and ponies. When one half of the field has been treated repeat the process with the other half.

Our particular pony, who happens to be very greedy, has a dreadful habit of always wanting to be where he should not, and when the rotational grazing plan was put into practice he would continually get through to the 'out of bounds' area. To keep him out the fencing has to be reinforced and he tested our patience to the very limit. For him it is always a case of 'The grass is greener on the other side of the fence'. You probably have a pony just like him.

Be careful also that in the spring, when the grass is lush, your pony does not have too much. Ponies, rather than horses, are notoriously greedy and will eat to bursting point if allowed to.

Unrestricted grazing on rich spring grass could cause laminitis, a disease of the feet caused by over-feeding. Grazing on good grass should be limited at that time of year, and on very good pasture right through until the end of the summer, by stabling the pony for most of the day (ensure that there is enough bedding and water for him). Regular exercise is also essential to help keep his weight down. Getting him fit gradually for the school summer holidays is essential, anyway.

In the summer your mount will also be plagued with flies, which generally buzz continually around his eyes. The only protection he has is his tail, which he can swish, hoping that the offending creatures will go away. They do not usually take that much notice, which is why I like to see at least two horses or ponies turned out together so that they can stand nose to tail and do each other a favour by keeping the flies at bay. But this is not always possible because you may not have the land to accommodate two. Remember, however, that fly repellents can be bought from any good saddler.

Apart from the fact that another horse will help out with the fly and insect problems, it is also good for any horse or pony to have some company. Standing in a field by himself all day, although enjoyable while he is eating, can get somewhat boring.

If you have the space available but do not have the services of another horse or pony you can always try turning a cow or cattle out with him. Horses are very selective eaters and leave the rank grass, whereas a cow will certainly gobble that up and get rid of any worm larvae which may have infested the pasture. I also know of one friend who turned a goat out with his daughter's pony which was fine but for the fact that it wanted to eat everything, including the trees, and his shirt, when he once left it off during a rather hot spell. However, goats do tend to butt people, and other animals.

In the early part of the year, January/February, when the

Mucking out should be done daily

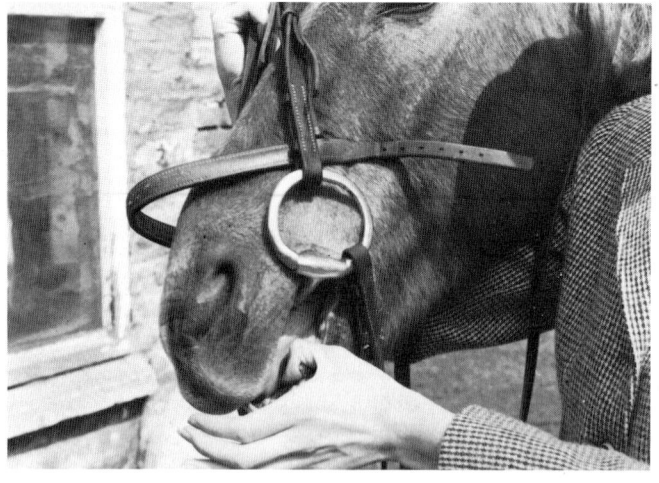

Be gentle when putting the bit in your pony's mouth

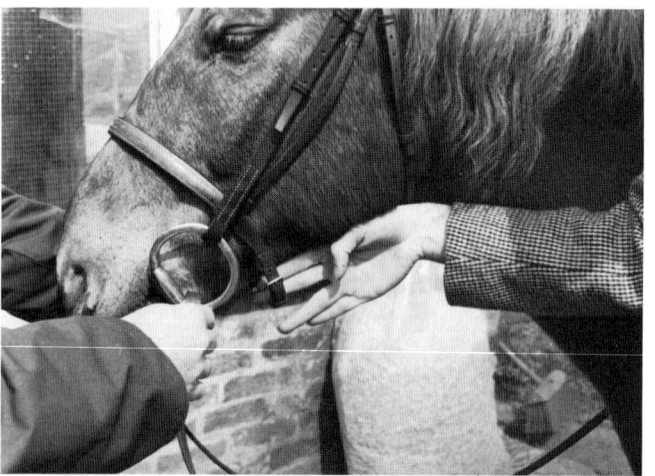

The noseband must fit correctly

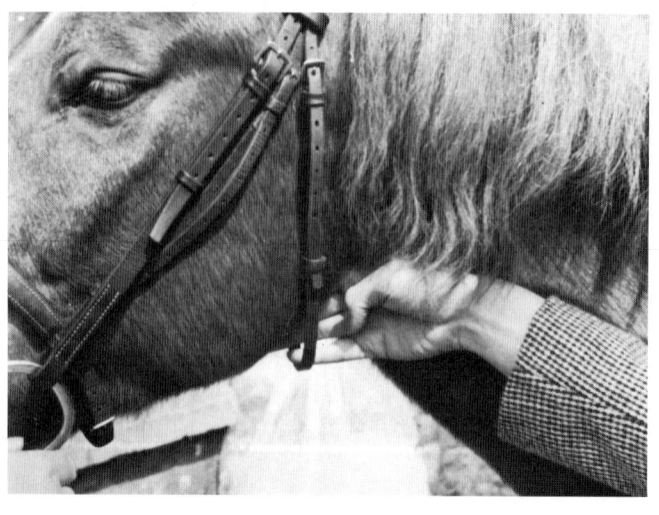

Never have the throat latch too tight

A strong headcollar is essential

Always use a quick release knot tied to string

Use rubber buckets when feeding

One of the best ways to carry a saddle

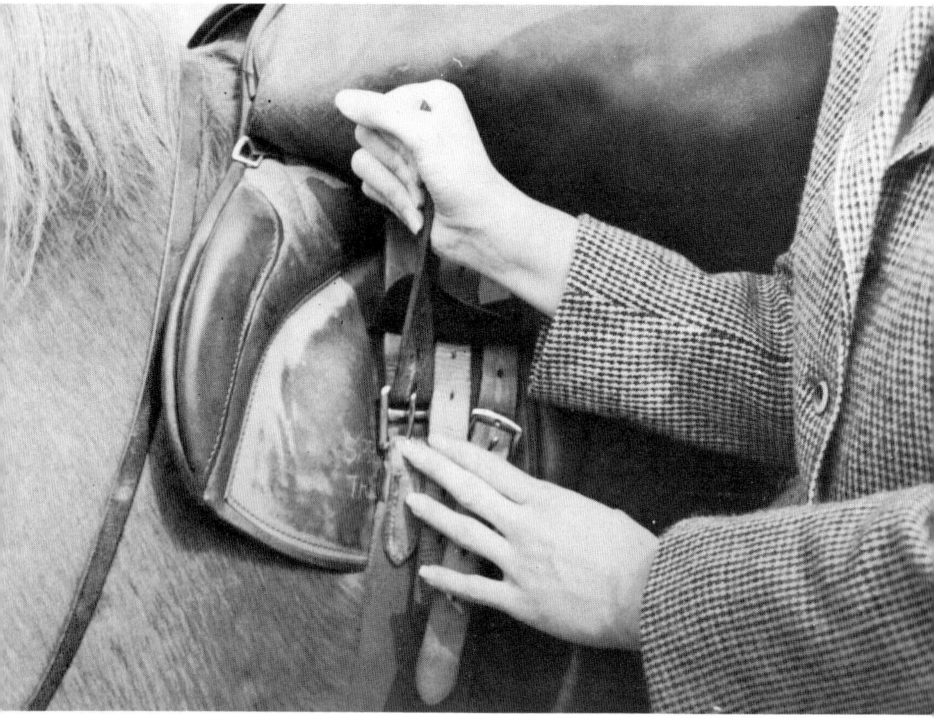

Check girth before and after mounting

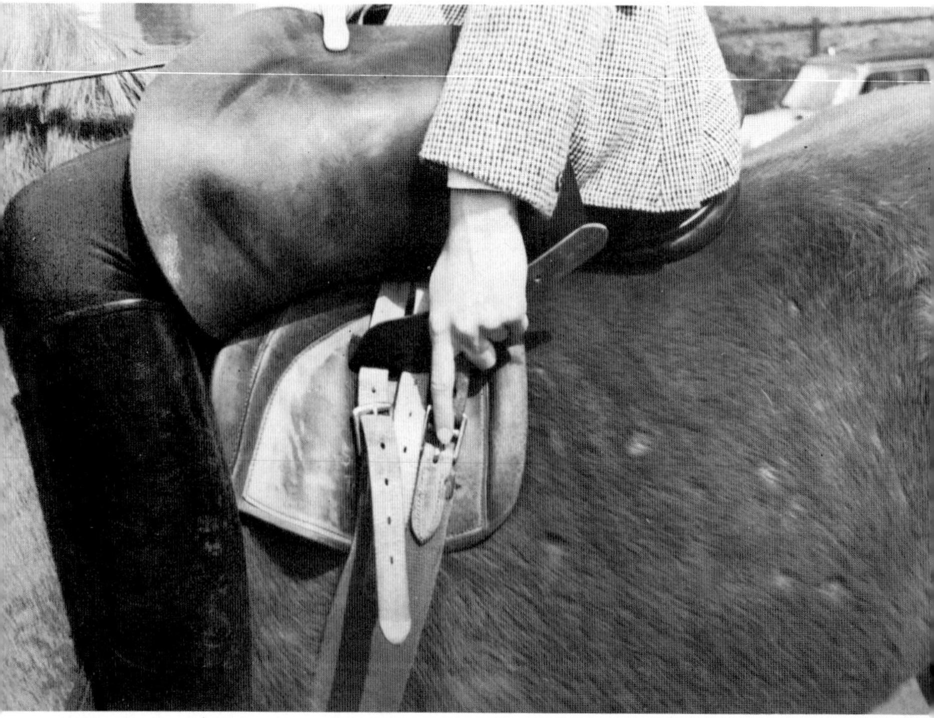

pony still has the long coat which has protected him through the winter, you will probably find some traces of lice. It sounds horrible, but, in fact, they can be got rid of with horse louse powder bought from a pet shop, tack shop or vet. Whether or not you find lice, you should treat your pony at this time of year. All you have to do is rub the powder into the coat and after a while the lice will go. Repeat the process after ten days. Practically every pony living has had lice at some stage or another, so do not go burying your head in shame and thinking that it is your fault when you actually find he has them. Getting rid of them is what matters most.

Later on in the season, about June or July time, you might also find him suffering from sweet itch which may perhaps sound nicer than lice but is a wretched condition. The pony rubs himself (usually his tail, or neck) because he itches incessantly and cannot get relief. Can you just imagine how it would feel? Sometimes the irritation is so great the animal will rub the affected part raw trying to stop the itching. Many people I have talked to consider that the condition is caused by an allergy to something in the grass. The vet might recommend a course of antihistamine injections and because the affected parts may be rubbed badly, he should advise ointment to be applied to ease the soreness. It is advisable, if there is any indication that the pony is a sweet itch sufferer (the previous owner should know) to ask the vet to prescribe preventive treatment *earlier* in the year.

You must persevere with the treatment until the condition has been cleared up to the vet's satisfaction. I know that calling in the vet is expensive but, although money can be saved in other areas, where the health of your horse or pony is concerned money must always come second to his needs. (See also chapter 11 on Ailments, page 127).

Warble flies are another problem that one may have to deal with during the summer months when they lay their yellow eggs on the pony's legs. The creatures eventually find their way into the animal's system and appear as lumps under the skin, usually on his back.

If the Warble is found on the saddle area the saddle must be left off until the creature has come out. It will eventually force its way through a hole it makes in the skin and fall off. Then you can clean the wound (treat it with wound powder) and the back will heal. If, however, you start trying to kill the things while they are developing under the skin, you will be plagued with problems. Any eggs on the pony's legs should be removed by scraping off with a pen-knife – but take care not to cut him or yourself.

Having read this particular chapter you will be forgiven for thinking that owning a pony is one continuous battle with all creatures great and small, who are ready to attack at any given moment to make your life a misery. Well, on occasions, that can be true, but you will find that the good times far outweigh the bad ones. Keeping a pony at grass, whatever else it does, will broaden your outlook. You will find and experience problems you never even knew existed but you will cope and be a better person for it.

Turning out your pony is just as important as catching him and if you make that a rushed job, you could find yourself in trouble. When you have the pony on the headcollar walk him through the gate and go several yards into the field, talking to him all the time. Then, slowly, turn him in a half-circle so that he is facing the way he came. Give him a tit-bit, rub him on the neck and then undo the headcollar buckle with the minimum of fuss and, still talking, walk away. Never turn out the pony with the headcollar on because he could get it caught up in something and do himself harm. Some people reading this will say, 'What on earth do I do if my pony is hard to catch but easier for me if I turn him out with a headcollar on?' The answer is simple 'Take it off and persevere.'

It does help, though, to be able to catch your pony once you have turned him out in the field, and it is not always as easy as it seems. The best thing to do is to talk to yourself or sing softly as you walk slowly up to him to put on the headcollar. The whole point of the exercise is to keep him calm and happy, so that when you want to catch him he will always allow himself to be caught. A good point to remember is that horses and ponies have superb memories and in particular, do not forget the bad things that happen to them.

If you go charging out into the field like a demented ape, waving the headcollar around, you will have little chance of catching your pony. Play safe, be sensible and always live to fight another day. What I call the 'easy action' always pays off in the long run. Never approach your pony as though you were walking through a freshly laid mine-field. Go straight towards him with a piece of carrot, or a sugar lump, so that he knows that if he is a good boy it is going to pay off.

It is not bribery, merely an action which could possibly save you a lot of time and energy and keep your pony much happier than he would be if he were chased all over the place. When you are a couple of strides from him stop and, still talking softly, offer him the tit-bit and see if he will amble over to you. Like hungry little boys, ponies always want something in their mouths and the temptation of a little sugar can sometimes work wonders.

Feed your pony or horse with the flat of the hand and, when he is concentrating only on what he is nibbling, gently put the headcollar on. But, whatever you do, do not practise any swift, sudden movements, otherwise he will probably set off like a rocket on its way to the moon. Even if he does, at the last moment, change his mind about being caught, do not lose your temper; just keep calm and be prepared for a fairly long session of tracking. Never run or start shouting because if you do he will resist you.

When your pony is turned out, depending on the weather and the state of the grass, you will need to feed him hay from about the start of November until May time.

Look at your pony every day when he is in the field and always remember to check his feet to see that his shoes are not too worn, or pinching. You will find, depending on the amount of work he is doing, that they will probably need replacing every four to six weeks. Even when he is not working, his feet grow.

And during the winter when it is cold and rainy he will also need to wear his New Zealand rug. Part of the point of you checking that he is okay each day is to make sure that the rug has not slipped and is hanging off him.

If your pony is in a field away from your house, where

members of the public can sometimes wander, make sure that the area where your mount is kept is free from tin cans and bottles. It is amazing how many people will walk in the country, enjoy it, and yet leave a long trail of rubbish upon which animals hurt themselves.

While you are searching for any debris also make sure that there are no pot holes in the paddock. If you find one, fill it in, otherwise your pony might gallop about, put a foot in it and damage a ligament. It only takes a quick look but it could save you so much trouble. Some people also have a habit of fiddling with gates, even though they know they should not, so check that the latch is secure, too.

When your pony has been out of work for some time because of dreadful weather, or because he has been ill, you must not make him charge about like a mad thing. Get him fit again slowly and surely, remember that he will tire, and that you must not overdo the amount of work you give him.

His muscles must be toned up again and if you try and do it all too quickly, he might pull one of them, after which it will take even longer to get him back to fitness. Patience is the key word. The surest way to make a horse or pony unhappy is to overwork him and ask him for the impossible.

Turn him sour and you will have destroyed what could have been a happy partnership.

5
Feeding

Feeding is a very complex subject, as each horse or pony has different needs depending on whether he lives in or out, the work he is doing and the amount and the quality of grass available to him at any given time. It is a very important subject and you must understand that overfeeding is just as bad as underfeeding. I do not believe anyone can advise you how much to give your mount when they have never seen him and do not know how much work he is doing each day. That is why I do not intend to provide you with charts which, in the end, could prove misleading. Those who do write about horses and ponies and do produce charts are full of good intentions but each horse and pony is an individual and should be treated as such, particularly where feeding is concerned.

This chapter is intended only as a guide – ideally, ask an experienced person in your area who knows the sort of pony you have and the work you are doing with him, to advise you on the exact amounts of food to give.

Firstly, the grass-kept pony. The amount of supplementary feed (that is, food given in addition to grass) depends largely on the time of year, and the weather. Let us begin with the month of October (or November, if the weather is still quite mild) when the pony must start to have hay once a day. You will probably be at school during the week, wrestling with the problems of Latin or maths, and will only ride at weekends and, therefore, you do not need to give him an actual feed. But he will need to have

Always feed him good food

between 3 and 7 pounds of hay each day, depending on his size.

When securing the haynet to the fence, tie it high enough to prevent him catching his hooves in it as it becomes less full and begins to sag. Alway use a quick release knot on string which is attached to the fence.

Alternatively, if several ponies are in the field, hay can be placed in piles spaced well apart, with one for each pony plus an extra portion to prevent a shy pony losing out if he is chased from his own food.

A cattle rack is useful for hay, too, and if there is one in the field, use it.

During December and January, when the pony will be going to rallies and generally working harder during the school Christmas holidays, a daily feed, and hay twice daily (6 to 14 pounds split between the two sessions) should be given. The feed should consist of chaff (which is chopped hay

Don't feed oats to excitable ponies

available from corn merchants in sacks), or bran. Oats can over-excite smaller ponies and, if that is the case with yours, do not feed them to him. Chaff and bran provide roughage and the former, in particular, helps to make the pony eat slowly and chew more, which is obviously beneficial. If he were to swallow the lot in one go, he might well be a suitable candidate for a bout of colic!

Oats are an energy food and can be fed bruised or rolled. As I have pointed out, some ponies should not be fed them because they do 'hot' them up and that can be dangerous if you are an inexperienced rider. It is best to consult your Pony Club instructor, or riding school proprietor, as to whether your PARTICULAR pony needs them or not. I put that word in capitals to emphasize the fact I am dealing with individual requirements.

Horse and pony cubes are a mixture of many different foods. They are sometimes fed alone, providing the staple diet for the animal, and they are less 'heating' than oats, but have a comparable nutritive value. However, many people feel that they make the pony's feed very uninteresting, and prefer to feed them in smaller quantities, along with other foods. Carrots can also be given in the feed, but remember to slice them longways, otherwise they may get caught in his throat and cause him to choke. I am a great believer in feeding carrots (at least 1 pound) as an extra because it helps make the animal's food much more interesting.

You should continue to give hay twice daily, as well as a feed, in February and March, as most ponies are at their lowest at this particular time of the year, and the grass will not have started to grow again. Also, you may be starting to get your pony fit for the Easter holidays, which are packed with Pony Club events and he will benefit from having a feed in addition to hay. Always keep a wary eye on the animal because his condition will tell you if you are feeding him too little, or too much. If you can see his ribs sticking out and his back looks like a hat-rack, then you are doing something very wrong and you must give him more food. If, on the other hand, he has a large belly which wobbles all over the place like a newly set jelly, you are giving him too much. It is all a question of common sense on your part.

Once the spring starts, however, the owner of any horse or pony must take care to prevent the animal becoming overfed. Reduce hay and feed until the grass is through when, providing there is an adequate amount in the field, hay can be cut out altogether. From May until the start of the summer holidays, if the grass is sufficient, the feed can also be cut out.

During the holidays, though, a feed must be given each day as the pony will be working hard and will probably be kept off the grass for long periods. He will be able to catch up with his bulk food at night, when he can graze, so hay is not really necessary. This feeding programme can be continued until the weather becomes colder again. Always remember, good food keeps the cold at bay.

There are several general rules when feeding a pony at grass and they should be strictly followed: (a) always feed at the same time each day because the pony will learn to expect you, and if several ponies are turned out together, it is inviting trouble to keep them waiting; (b) once you have started on a feeding programme, stick to it and, if you are forced to change it, do so very gradually to prevent the pony's digestive system from being upset; (c) only use the best quality foodstuffs; (d) provide clean, fresh water because a pony cannot keep his condition without it. If you stick to these rules your horse or pony will, without doubt, be well looked after, and will not suffer any hardship.

Be slap-happy about everything, though, and the relationship between you and your mount will sour in no time at all. Such behaviour will show very clearly that you are lazy and have no right to be an owner and take on the responsibilities it entails.

Now, it is time to deal with the stabled pony and the first thing to make a note of is that a pony or a horse who is kept in a loose box will be consuming less grass in twenty-four hours, even if he is turned out most of the day, than one kept at grass all night. Therefore, he must be given supplementary food to make up for this. I will assume that the pony is turned out, or ridden and then turned out, after his morning feed, and brought in for his evening one. Personally, I consider it wrong, and unnecessary, to stable a pony both day and night. In my view a period each day in the field is essential to his well-being.

To keep him going through the night he will need a haynet, securely tied to string on the special ring in his stable. (You should never tie anything, whether it be the pony or a haynet straight to the metal ring; attach string first. This is to help prevent accidents should the horse pull back suddenly or become caught up.)

Continuing with the feeding programme, he will need 7 to 12 pounds of hay, depending on his size (small ponies are not usually stabled, therefore those amounts are calculated for larger ones).

Put the haynet in as late at night as possible, so that he does not have to wait too long between finishing the hay and eating his morning feed. Unless the animal is in very hard work, he will require just two feeds a day. These should consist of oats or barley and horse and pony cubes, chaff or bran, plus carrots. As is the case for grass-kept ponies, the exact amount of each feed depends so much on individual animals, the type of work they are doing, their height and, sometimes, their temperament and that, again, means it is impossible for me to give you exact amounts for your particular animal. Once again you will have to consult the Pony Club instructor, District Commissioner or senior member of your local riding school. You may also be helped by the pony's previous owner and, providing the pony is in good condition, and doing the same amount of work with you as he was with the person from whom you bought him, and grazing comparable pasture, it is wise to stick to the feeding programme he is used to.

As well as the basic foods, there are some variations which can be given to stable ponies. For example, to add variety flaked maize can be fed occasionally, in place of some of the animal's usual ration of oats. Also molasses (watered down and sprinkled on the feed) can be given (again, amounts depend on each individual). They are tasty and of high nutritional value.

There are various additives and supplements on the market, but these should really only be fed on the vet's instructions, as a pony or horse receiving adequate amounts of good quality foodstuffs should be getting all the minerals and vitamins that he needs.

It is useful to know how to make a bran mash, as after a busy show, hunter trial or all-day rally, when your pony may be too tired to digest a normal feed, it is a good substitute. It needs very little digesting and is easy to eat. To make the bran mash, boil some water and pour enough onto about half a bucket of bran to make it wet, but not sloppy. Mix well, cover with a cloth and leave until just warm. If it is too hot the pony will either burn himself, or not eat at all. A small quantity of oats can be mixed in to replace some of the pony's lost energy and make the feed a little more interesting than it might otherwise be. Sliced carrots (lengthways) can also be added.

When you are feeding your pony offer him a drink before he eats, because this cuts down the chances of his getting colic, due to the food being washed through the stomach too quickly.

If you are looking after your mount properly, you will notice any sudden change in his eating habits, and if he is a good 'doer' who, for no reason at all (as far as you know) starts picking at his food or leaving it, you must find out very quickly what the problem is. The first thing to check is his teeth. Sometimes they develop very rough edges which cut his cheeks and tongue when he eats and, therefore, he will not be encourged to chew while that is happening.

Once you have ascertained that his teeth do need some attention (and when you are looking do not let him bite your fingers) you will have to summon the vet, who will rasp the rough edges away and make the animal feel better all round. You might discover that his teeth are not sharp at all in which case he might well be suffering from a dental condition which also needs care. Again, the vet will have to be called.

Always make a point of checking his teeth at regular intervals and then you will know that all is well. To look into the pony's mouth, put your thumb on one side and your fingers of the same hand on the opposite side and press onto the bars of the mouth, as you would when putting his bit in.

Another reason why your pony might not be eating properly is because he is suffering from lampas, a condition whereby the roof of the mouth drops to the level of the teeth which makes eating painful. My own children's pony suffered from lampas and the vet suggested that we sprinkle an ounce of salt in each feed which, I must say, did a great deal of good. This is a fine alternative for a pony who is not interested in a salt lick (a block of salt) which is usually fixed to the wall of the stable in its own holder. Some horses love to lick them while others, like ours, will not entertain them at all.

He has a great liking for parsnips, though, and our local greengrocer makes sure we have an ample supply. This proves my point that people will always help out if they know that your children have a pony. It is much appreciated by us and our pony, Squirrel. But although he is also partial to a large juicy carrot, we do not make a habit of filling him up with tit-bits because he might expect them at the wrong times and, the chances are, nip us if we decided he should go without.

He usually has his parsnips (cut lengthways) when he is caught in the field and they are fed with the flat of the hand.

Some ponies who live in have a dreadful habit of charging for their food when it is being given and you must cure them of that otherwise they might hurt you in their rush to the manger. Be kind but firm and do not let him take any liberties with you. If he can get away with it once, he will try again. And, as you are probably aware, that is not always in the pony's interest.

Ponies are much bigger and stronger than you are and, believe me, it does hurt if they push against you or, even worse, tread on your feet, particularly when you have wellington boots on and your feet are cold! The mere thought sends shivers down my spine as it has happened to me in the past. If you can avoid it, do! There is a very old saying that you learn by your mistakes. I have found it is much better to learn by the ones other people make – it is less painful!

Another good point to remember is that you should try and be quiet when you are feeding your mount. Having something to munch is what he thoroughly enjoys and to have someone jumping up and down while he is doing so might lead to him getting annoyed and angry enough to kick out. You like to enjoy your food – well so does he. Also, while on the subject, do not treat him like a circus horse and ask him to do tricks like taking sweets out of your mouth. It is highly dangerous and very unhygienic. I knew a young man who would sit in between his horse's forelegs and encourage him to take a mint from his own mouth. He thought it was clever at the time until the horse nibbled his nose in mistake for the sweet! It was a trick he never tried again and rightly so, because it was unnecessary and stupid. In fact, I do not agree at all with the feeding of sweets to ponies or horses because it is bad for their teeth.

While on the subject of feeding, I should mention Complete Cubes which, as the name implies, incorporate all your mount will need, including hay, and can therefore be fed without anything else. But again while some animals adore them others find them dry and do, perhaps, need to drink more water. Some also find them boring and, anyway, I like to see my pony eating hay because, as far as I am concerned, that is part of his enjoyment of life. It is, however, a question of choice and must be left to each owner to decide.

Remember that it is a false economy to buy cheap foodstuffs because they will not do your pony as much good as the more expensive feeds. I know everyone has to watch how much they spend but on food, as with treatment of illness, you must not take any short cuts. For example, if you were to buy cheap, dusty hay that did not smell sweet, you would find that it was not good value and had very little to recommend it. If your horse or pony suffers from a dust allergy, he might also find himself in bad trouble with his breathing.

Even if you buy expensive hay, it can still, sometimes, be dusty and if your horse is allergic to dust, it is wise to soak the hay well in water before feeding.

There are many types of hay but the ones you will probably be buying are seed hay and meadow hay. Seed hay contains several types of grasses, including clover, rye and sanfoin and, if it is of good quality, it will smell sweet. Meadow hay is cut from permanent pasture-land and, ideally, should be about seven months old before being fed. Again, like seed hay, the meadow variety should smell sweet or, in the words of country people who know what they are talking about, should have a good 'nose'.

6
Grooming

Every morning before you leave your house you will have washed, brushed your teeth and put on clean clothes. The object of the exercise is to keep clean and healthy. If you did not bother you would probably feel dreadful and could become unwell. Horses and ponies are the same as humans in this respect. If they are stabled they need grooming daily to circulate the blood and to maintain condition and health.

I will deal with the stabled pony first because although ponies who live out also need grooming, the principles behind it are different. They have to protect themselves against wind, rain and snow and need to retain the natural oils in their coats. A good, vigorous grooming would stimulate the glands which produce the oil as a result of which your pony would stand the chance of losing that natural product and, consequently, the water-proofing it provides.

For the stabled pony, however, the routine is different, since he does not roll in the field when he wants to and, therefore, cannot stimulate his own muscles or glands. He relies on you to do it for him.

After tying a rope attached to his headcollar to the appropriate ring using a quick release knot, lift up each of his feet and, using a hoof-pick, clean them out quickly and efficiently. Run the hook of the pick around the inner rim of the shoe and down the hoof from the frog to toe, lift out the mud and then gently work out any rubbish which has collected along the cleft of the frog (the rubbery looking substance on the sole which is shaped like a 'V' and acts as a shock absorber and anti-slip device). Do not dig the hoof-pick into the frog.

Once you have removed the dung and mud from the hooves put it in a skep. If you leave it lying around the animal will only stand on it again when moving about. When this has been done, take the skep and place it outside the stable while you are grooming otherwise you, or the horse or pony might knock it over.

Your grooming kit should consist of a dandy brush, body brush, three curry combs (metal, rubber, plastic), a hoof-pick, sponges (two), stable rubbers (two), a water brush and a sweat scraper. Ideally, you should keep them in a draw-string canvas bag, or a properly designed grooming tray, which has a handle and is easy to carry. You should also have hoof oil and brush kept in a protective bag so that it does not make everything else greasy.

A dandy brush should not be used on the tail, head or mane, but does a fine job of brushing thick layers of dried mud off horses who have been spending their time rolling while turned out. Some horses and ponies seem able to home in on a mud patch even when there has been a drought. Make a note that dandy brushes should not be used on very ticklish animals or clipped-out ponies who live in.

The body brush is much softer than the dandy. Its purpose is to remove grease, scurf and dust from the pony's body and legs and to brush the head, mane and tail. If you were to use a dandy brush on the animal's head, the bristles might hurt him, particularly where the skin stretches over the face.

One of the reasons why I suggest you keep three curry combs is that each has a different function. The metal one is to help clean the body brush while it is in use, the plastic one takes off caked mud and the rubber curry comb is ideal for helping to remove excess hair when the animal is changing its coat. They are not expensive items to buy and do come in very handy. The hoof-pick's function I have explained. The reason you need two sponges is a matter of hygiene. One is required to clean the pony's mouth, nose and eyes and the other is used to sponge down his dock (the area under the tail). If you had only a single sponge, even if you rinsed it regularly, there would be a chance of cross-infection, something which is eradicated by using separate sponges.

Two, or even three stable rubbers (something similar to a tea-towel) are always useful. They are used on stable ponies, and grass-kept ponies (only in the summer) to give their coats an extra shine, but they do become dirty very quickly. So if you have several in your bag, there is always a clean one at hand while the others are being washed and dried.

The water brush should be used only, in my opinion, on the mane and tail. I do not like the same piece of equipment being dipped into a bucket in order to wash off mud from the hooves. Again, this item is not expensive and, anyway, once bought, will last for ages if it is looked after. The simple answer is to buy two; mark one with a sign so that it is used only on the mane and tail and the other with a large 'H' for the hooves. I will not advise you to use a wisp (a pad made of twisted straw) because to make one with straw, when you are using wood-shavings in your stable, is somewhat difficult.

Even though a several-times folded stable-rubber can be substituted, it is not really necessary for young people who probably have older, first ponies. Start thumping away at their aged muscles in order to tone them up and they would begin asking themselves what on earth you were doing. You can promote ample circulation by good, vigorous grooming with brushes, and while some people might like to thump away at race-horses, eventers and hunters with a wisp, personally I do not think it of vital importance to an old, first pony.

The sweat scraper is, as its name implies, an implement to take off sweat from the body and neck (but not from grass-kept ponies), and is also ideal for removing excess water after bathing the stabled horse. It is half-moon shaped, with a rubber covering over metal.

One important point to remember is to allow yourself plenty of time for grooming. If you organize it properly it can be enjoyed by you and the horse or pony. It also needs to be done methodically, so that parts of the coat are not missed. Be warned now that the biggest thing that might put you off grooming at first is fatigue. During the first week you will probably feel as though your arms are about to fall off and that some invisible karate expert has been aiming blows at your stomach with the sole intention of hurting every muscle you have. You will need to get used to the constant routine and, once you have, those aching limbs will soon be forgotten. You will become fitter day by day until you reach a level when you do not even think about tired arms. It is all well worth it for both you and your mount. But you must persevere.

To start off with you should allow at least an hour to groom him and for the stabled pony I would suggest you begin the work after he has returned from his exercise. Before taking him out you should have tidied him up, brushing mane and tail, picking out feet as described earlier and cleaning off any stable marks. But the real grooming, which he will thoroughly appreciate, starts on your return.

To begin, tie the pony again to the short rack ring with a rope attached to his headcollar, pick out the feet in case there are any pebbles jammed between the frog and the inner rim of the shoe, and check that he has not stepped on a nail or any other sharp object. Both, if not removed, can cause a lot of pain and, on many occasions, lameness. Being vigilant can prevent a lot of trouble later on.

When you have completed that job, pick up the dandy brush and clean off any dried, crusted sweat but do not use this particular brush on the mane or the tail. You might think it is ideal for untangling knots of hair but what it in fact does do, if you are not careful, is split the hair strands and cause some of them to fall out because the bristles of the brush are rather harsh. If you find tangles, separate them with your fingers and then brush them out properly with the body brush.

Once you have finished with the dandy start to groom the pony with the body brush; beginning with the nearside (left) of the headcollar strap, slip it off his nose and do the strap up around his neck. Be careful and gentle when handling his head. Some animals do not like their ears being touched or pulled about.

They have to be done, of course, but do not rush in like a bull in a china shop because he might become frightened, pull back on the headcollar and snap the rope. He might even tread on you in the process, which is not at all pleasant and to be avoided at all costs! While you are smoothly brushing his face, talk to the pony all the time – about the weather, what you had for breakfast, or how much you like your best friend at school – it does not really matter as long as it is soothing and has a calming effect on him. I am sure if you spoke to him in Chinese, he would not mind. The whole idea is to keep him happy while you work and, when you think about it, it is rather pleasant for you, too.

When you have finished the head, undo the headcollar strap and place it back where it was originally. Then clean your body brush with the metal curry comb by running the latter through the bristles several times.

After this has been done put your left hand through the brush's strap and, using half-circular rhythmic movements, start grooming his neck and shoulders, blowing slowly through your lips to prevent yourself from swallowing the dust and scurf which will come out of his coat. Brush under the neck, over the chest and work your way round to the side of the shoulder. While you are doing this your right hand should be resting on the nearside of his back so that you keep physical contact with him. When you start to groom the inside of his off-fore transfer the brush to your right hand and, holding the outside of the leg with your left hand, begin to smooth the hair with the brush, being careful not to hit the chestnut (the horny growth inside the hind and front legs at hock or knee level).

When the grooming of the leg has been completed, transfer the brush to your other hand again and concentrate on his withers, back and stomach. Remember to clean the brush at regular intervals and, when you brush under your pony's tummy, be extremely careful. He might be ticklish and, if he is, he might just lift his near-hind leg up to kick you – not with any malice aforethought, but even so, if he connects it will jolly well hurt.

After grooming his quarters with firm, semi-circular

strokes, push him over and start the process again, remembering to talk to him and give him a pat occasionally. While you are using the body brush keep on running the curry comb through it to rid the bristles of dust and dirt.

Also work on the mane and tail with this particular brush and if you find the tail has become tangled during the night, separate the strands of hair with your fingers. When you are doing this stand to the side of the pony, no matter how safe you think he is. Just ease the tail round to the nearside of his rump and brush downwards quickly but firmly. The reason you should not stand directly behind him is that even if he is safe something might startle him, and he could kick out at you. It is always better to be safe than sorry and if you think about what you are doing beforehand there is every chance you will go through your equestrian life unscathed.

When you have sorted out the mane and tail, dip the water brush in the bucket and just dampen the crest of his neck and top of his tail to spruce him up a bit.

I am a firm advocate of sponging the animal's dock, eyes and nose each day. When you perform these tasks, do not leave him dripping with water. First make sure the water is warm – you only need to use your imagination to know what would happen if you slapped a spongeful of cold water over his bottom when he was not expecting it. He might leap two feet in the air and land back on you.

Then squeeze out what I call the rump sponge in the warm water, lift his tail (once again standing by his side) and wipe the dock area clean. Normally it is not too messy but, even if it is, the job has to be done, so take a deep breath and get on with it. It is no different in theory from changing a baby's nappy and when it is done it is much better for all concerned. When you are sponging the dock, if you notice any nicks or cuts, put a dab of antiseptic cream on them to prevent the pony becoming sore and uncomfortable.

Afterwards rinse out the sponge in clean water, wash your hands, change the water in the bucket and, using the face sponge, wipe his eyes and nostrils clean, making sure you do not pull out the 'feeler' hairs in his nose. When all this has been done, you will probably feel tired. Have a short rest

When cleaning dock please use warm water

before moving down to his feet – by this time you will have deserved it.

The feet should have been picked out earlier and washed and now it is just a question of lifting up each foot and putting hoof oil on it. When you are doing the nearside of the horse or pony the tin containing the oil is placed just a short way from your right leg, where it is easy to reach but hard for him to knock over and make a mess of his bed. Reverse the process for the offside. Wipe the brush around the wall of the hoof from the coronet band down to the toe. The hoof is made of horn and the application of oil once a day not only makes it look clean and healthy but promotes growth as well and stops it becoming dry and brittle.

There is a very old saying which has been handed down over the years: 'No foot no oss' and it is very true. The feet must be taken good care of and no effort should be spared when working on them.

Some people suggest that car engine oil be applied to the hooves, but the proper oil for horses' feet is sold fairly cheaply and I would recommend that you stick to that.

Having discussed the stabled pony and the part grooming plays, we must also know how to go about looking after animals who live out in fields in all weathers, during winter and summer. This is not such a hard job because, as I mentioned earlier, they need to retain the grease in their coats to keep out the bad weather.

Bring the pony up from the field, tie him up with a rope attached to his headcollar and, if he is wet, dry his saddle patch by rubbing the way the hair lies with a stable rubber, towel or handfuls of straw, if available. Pick out his feet, brush his mane and tail with a body brush (or just leave them if wet) and then remove any mud with the dandy.

Before taking him on a ride make sure there is no mud or dried sweat on his saddle patch, where the bridle touches and the area where his girth goes. If you do not remove it, he could return with rub marks on his skin which can be painful and should never be allowed to occur. When his feet have been picked out and washed, paint hoof oil on them, unless it is very muddy, in which case it will just rub off as soon as you set out.

If your pony lives out wearing a New Zealand rug but comes back from a ride wet, cover his back with a layer of straw, (this procedure is called 'thatching'), put an anti-sweat rug over the top, followed by an *old* jute rug upside down, then leave him to dry. His usual rug can then be put on about two hours later. Do not leave him standing in wet rugs though, after he has dried, as this could give him a chill. This method can also be used when a stabled pony comes in wet from a ride and needs to have his rugs put on later in the day.

While you are grooming keep a watchful eye open for any cuts or bruises on his body, particularly if he lives out with several other ponies. You very nearly always find one who turns out to be a bully, who will kick or bite just because the fancy takes him. That may be all right if he does not become really vicious, but even if he just nips his so-called friends it can prove painful and may cause health problems if wounds are not treated.

If you discover a small cut on his leg, do not worry, just bathe it clean with salt water and apply wound powder to keep away any germs. You might even come across the odd lump or two, or swelling. If the skin has not been broken just treat with cold water to encourage the puffiness to go down. If any deepish cuts are discovered then it is best to seek immediate veterinary advice because it is not worth taking any chances.

While on this subject, remember the importance of keeping the animal's anti-tetanus injections up to date. He should have been having a primary course of injections with a booster every year.

Do not think that because you cannot see any cuts the injections are unnecessary. Undetected puncture wounds are even more susceptible to tetanus infection. With the right course of preventative treatment, however, there will be no need for you to worry and it is best to ask the advice of your local vet. Once your horse or pony has started the course, it is easy for you to keep a record thereafter.

Tetanus is caused by bacteria entering the bloodstream and very few horses survive once they have been infected. So always make sure that you keep the animal's veterinary health notes up to date. Tetanus injections are not expensive and do not hurt when administered. In fact, half the time the ponies do not even know when they have been given them because they are so quick and painless.

I would also advise that if you own a pony or horse, or work with them, you too should have an anti-tetanus jab. Every member of my family has taken that precaution and I rest easy in the knowledge that, even if they are bitten, or cut themselves, they are protected against tetanus.

All you have to do is go and make an appointment with your doctor and, if he cannot give you the injection himself, he will refer you to the local hospital. I went along one day and was in and out within ten minutes, not having felt a thing. It is simple and makes for safer living. There may be times, no matter how careful you are, when accidents happen and you may receive a kick, or a cut and you, too, will want to be protected.

After checking that your pony is all right and having prepared him, saddle up and go off on your ride. Remember, however, that once you have returned from exercise you must look at his feet again and if they need picking out, do just that.

This is not only to find out if he has picked up any stones but to see if the actual shoes are still firmly on his feet.

Sometimes they can be half torn off by slipping on the road, or another pony bumping into the back of him during the ride or by walking through thick mud. If the shoe is hanging off remove it if you know how or call the farrier. Otherwise the nails could puncture the soles of the hoof and then you will have real trouble because the animal will almost certainly go lame.

If he does, he will need constant care, you will not be able to ride him and your veterinary bills will rise so rapidly your parents will think that they are paying a second mortgage. All of this can be avoided if you follow the basic rules of horse and pony ownership and think constructively about everything you do.

If you have to remove any of the shoes (and you should not

attempt it unless you have been shown the correct way by your blacksmith), remember not to leave them lying about the place. Place it, or them, in a box and ask the blacksmith to come and put new ones on as soon as he can. Horses should not be ridden without shoes.

The blacksmith is worth his weight in gold, as will be seen in a later chapter in this book, and you must treat him with the respect he deserves. Without him we would all be badly off since half the time it is his expertise which saves our ponies from having serious trouble with their feet. He will strike up a friendly relationship with your pony, who will eventually trust him without a second thought. And the blacksmith will get to know him so well he will be able to make his shoes from memory.

7
The tack

Although there are quite a few types of saddles, the ones that will really be of interest to you are the general purpose, dressage, jumping and show jumping saddles unless, of course, you intend to be a jockey or spend your life playing polo!

You are unlikely, in the early part of your equestrian life, to use anything other than a general pupose saddle but you may also be interested in being able to identify dressage, jumping and showing saddles, so I will mention only these and not bog you down with information about unusual types.

As I have said, the best and most useful saddle when you are first starting out is the general purpose one which is, as its name implies, used for all sorts of riding including jumping and dressage at all but the most advanced levels. It is only when you become besotted by a specialist equestrian pastime that you need to think of dressage, show jumping, or show saddles, and by that time either your parents will have resigned themselves to the fact that your hobby is going to cost them a great deal of money, or you will be earning a living and be able to pay for it all yourself.

The saddles that show jumpers use are designed with the side flaps cut forward. This is so that the rider has plenty of leather to grip with his knees when adopting the forward position necessary for negotiating obstacles. Although this is the type of seat used by the majority, there are a few show jumping riders who make mockery of the practicalities of

Don't copy outrageous riding styles

design with outrageous riding styles. I know of at least two whose knees come right off the saddle when they are jumping. They should not be copied, as most people who tried to ride in this way would end up saying hello to the sawdust on the arena floor.

The dressage saddle is as different from the jumping one as chalk is from cheese, because the rider needs to be in the middle of the saddle right over the horse's centre of gravity. It has a much straighter flap, bringing the rider as close as possible to his horse.

The dressage competitor must not lose contact with his mount at any time. And anyone who has seen the beautifully timed and executed displays by Switzerland's Christine Stuckelberger on Granat, or Austria's Elisabeth Theurer on Mon Chérie, will have an idea of the importance of this.

The side panels on showing saddles are, if anything, cut even straighter than their dressage counterpart because the judges need to see as much of the horse as possible.

There is also evidence that side-saddle riding is coming back into fashion which is rather interesting. In the old days ladies would no more have dreamed of riding astride than they would of smoking cigars in public. Now, however, times have changed.

The side-saddle is designed so that the rider can sit comfortably with both legs on the same side. There are two pommels fixed to it to afford the lady as much comfort as possible and to give her something to grip with her right leg. I have always considered that this type of riding crystallises the elegance and beauty of a much missed time in our history.

But by far the most important point to remember is that fitting a saddle properly, no matter what discipline you are using it for, is essential because a badly fitting one can cause a lot of damage to the pony's or horse's back. To avoid this make sure that the front arch of the saddle is not too high or too low. The best way to judge this is to mount and then check that you can put your fingers between the withers and the top of the front arch and that you can see from front to back along the gullet. Make sure that when you buy the saddle it is the correct size, neither too wide nor too narrow. It should not pinch or rub the withers. If it does it will take some of the skin off and make him dreadfully sore. And, because of the position of the injury, superficial as it may be it will take ages to heal. Very narrow topped horses suffer from this problem and extra care should be taken to stop the saddle pressing down on, or pinching the skin.

When the saddle has been put on, make sure there is no pressure on the spine or loins. If the weight is evenly distributed and the girth done up properly so that the saddle is not rocking about like a badly sprung perambulator, all will be well. Do the girth up before you mount and then, once you are in the saddle, pull it up another hole to make sure it is secure. Some horses and ponies blow themselves out when you first tighten the girth. Then when you mount the tummy goes back to its normal size, leaving you with a slack girth and, consequently, in a vulnerable situation.

Remember, too, that when you are first putting the girth into position you must not let the leather, webbing, nylon or lampwick tuck up small folds of skin, so that it rubs sore during the ride. Everything must be placed firmly and securely but comfortably.

I will continue dealing with the saddle first because it is the most expensive piece of equipment you will buy as far as tack is concerned. Although some people call saddlery tackle, that particular word is not for me because, for obvious reasons, I think of fishing when I hear it. Therefore I try to avoid it if possible and stick to tack.

Apart from the necessity of fitting your horse or pony properly, the saddle must also be suitable for your needs. If, for example, you have rather a large bottom (which is nothing to be ashamed of) it will need to be sat upon something big enough so that you are comfortable. Failure to take these points into account would almost certainly lead to your suffering from a sore rear-end. To give you an example it would be comparable to an overweight cowboy trying to ride the range in a saddle designed for a jockey like Lester Piggott. Always look and be comfortable when riding. It will be best for you and the horse.

The first saddle my children ever owned was bought second-hand and gave them good, reliable service for several years before being replaced by a new one. But it did fit the pony and them properly and was, for an old saddle, very good value.

When buying a second-hand saddle, however, you must make sure that the tree (frame) is not cracked or broken. Ask a saddler to inspect it for you before you buy privately. If there is not one available in your area, or there is and he refuses to help, seek advice from an experienced member of the local riding school. One of the tell-tale signs of a damaged tree is crinkled leather on the seat of the saddle. Another test worth trying is to hold the front arch of the saddle with the left hand and the centre with the right hand and try and bend them towards each other. If there is more than a little 'give' there is a possibility that the tree is broken or damaged.

One thing to be aware of though is that in a spring-tree saddle there will be a slight flexing across the seat which is not present in a rigid tree saddle. Do not confuse that with any damage. But if you are doubtful seek further advice.

A saddle must fit correctly

Also check that the stitching on the main body of the saddle has not worn and that the girth straps are still in good condition. You might find adverts extolling the virtues of a 'new' type of leather which can be produced on the outer edges of the moon at a fraction of the cost of ordinary leather. Leather for safe saddles and bridles is not cheap so do not be led into buying inferior goods: it will probably cost you a lot more in the long run.

Having written about the saddle, I now want to introduce you to the girths, which hold it in place on the animal's back. There are several types and those you will be interested in, are the lampwick, nylon (or string), leather or webbing ones. Personally, I prefer the lampwick types because they lay comfortably on the horse and are easy to clean. They are also less likely to rub and cause girth galls (sore swellings).

Leather girths are also very good but need constant care to keep them soft. Nylon ones are cheaper but sometimes tend to pinch, as do string girths. Webbing girths are used two at a time because one might break and for that reason I would choose an alternative.

Apart from the material from which girths are made, one must also check that they are the right length. They should come about half way up the girth straps when tightened. If they are too long, the saddle could slip, rubbing the pony's back. You could even fall off and get hurt. You must also remember to ensure that no skin is pinched when the girth is tightened. To prevent this, pull each foreleg forward in turn, gripping the leg just below the knee, then run your finger underneath the girth to straighten out the skin. Before all this you should have cleaned the area of dried sweat and the small mud balls which have a habit of collecting and sticking underneath the tummy, particularly of grass-kept ponies.

The next vital appendage to the saddle are the stirrup leathers and irons which must be of high quality. Look after them properly like the rest of your tack, firstly for safety's sake and secondly to save money. When using the leathers you will obviously have them at a length suitable to the length of your legs whereby you can grip properly and feel comfortable. Remember, however, to adjust that length as the leather stretches. Swap the leathers on to the other side occasionally to prevent the one on the nearside (the side you mount) from becoming longer than the other.

The stirrup irons should not be too big or too tiny for your feet. If they are too large your feet might slip through and if they are too small your feet might get stuck in them. Ideally there should be 1 centimetre either side of the boot. Do not ride in anything but the correct footwear, which has been specifically designed with comfort and safety in mind.

Looking on the black side, I have always thought it desirable with so much metal about to have rubber treads fitted to one's irons. These serve a dual purpose: (a) they stop your feet slipping, and (b) if lightning happened to strike there is more chance of your surviving it while touching rubber. The chances of that happening are extremely remote because you should not be riding when lightning is about, but it is possible for a storm to blow up out of nothing and I am just being cautious.

The bridle is, of course, as essential as the saddle because unless you are riding a circus horse who turns, stops, goes forwards, sideways and backwards, on command of leg and hand movements, you cannot ride without one. I get very angry when I see people treating horses' mouths badly because there simply is no need for such stupid behaviour. The animal's mouth, like yours, has nerves and feeling and if you start tugging on it and using the bridle like a chainsaw, you could cause untold damage. Too many horses' and ponies' mouths have been ruined by people with hands resembling butchers' meathooks and a brain the size of an undersized pea. You should be able to feel the horse in your hands and he will trust you if you are not jabbing the bars of his mouth with a stainless steel bit every time you want him to stop. If you do, his character will eventually be destroyed because you will frighten him; he will become difficult to manage and will end up having a mouth that has lost all feeling and is about as soft as a cast-iron bar. If that happens you are a suitable candidate to spend three months mucking out, not riding, with no time off for good behaviour.

The best thing to do is be generous and learn how to ride

Jodhpurs should look good and feel right

Grooming kit should be kept clean and tidy. Shown here are a) soft body brush, b) rubber curry comb, c) stable cloth, d) metal curry comb, e) dandy brush, f) water brush, g) hoof pick. Other necessary items include sponges, plastic curry comb and sweat scraper.

Pick out hooves and frog before and after riding

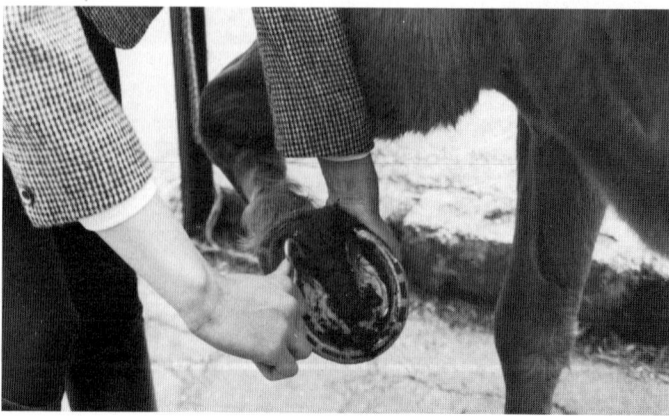

Stand to one side and use body brush to groom tail

Oil feet regularly to keep clean and promote growth of hoof

Pony Club members always look smart in the saddle

properly, because it is much more fun. Also it is always best to consult an expert about what sort of bit your pony should have and how to fit it.

There are several types of bridles but the ones which are most likely to be of interest to you are the eggbutt snaffle, Kimblewick and Pelham. They are not harsh on a horse if fitted properly and unlikely to do any damage. When buying a bridle make sure the leather is in excellent condition and that the bit is the right size for your mount. A snaffle bit should, ideally, protrude 0.5 centimetres each side of the mouth. And, when you have fitted it, it should just lie on the bars of the mouth (the area of gum between the front and back teeth) without being too high or too low. Of the bits I have mentioned, I prefer the eggbutt snaffle which is not too severe. It is a fixed ring jointed snaffle which prevents pinching at the corner of the mouth. This is an ideal bit for young riders whose hands are not, perhaps, as light as they should be.

The Kimblewick, which has a curb chain, gives additional control and is useful on strong ponies, but it can be severe if not properly adjusted. Remember when fitting this bridle that the curb chain must be twisted right-handed until it lies flat in the chin groove.

The Pelham has a single mouthpiece but two reins and should only be used by more experienced riders who have been taught how to handle two reins. It is useful to be able to identify it at shows, however.

There are many other types of bits but I intend only to deal with those which are generally used every day, so that your head does not swim with information which you cannot use at this stage, anyway. Apart from having the right bit for your particular mount, you should also know how to fit a bridle properly. It is no use having one thing right and six others wrong.

When the bridle is in one piece, ease the bit into the horse's mouth, then fit the headpiece across the top of the head behind the ears; you will then be able to check to see if the bit is correctly placed in the mouth. Remember, if it is too low he will get his tongue over the top and, if it is too high, you will hurt his mouth. If it needs altering, move the cheekpieces up or down a hole or two.

The noseband must lie two fingers' width below the bottom of the cheekbone and you must be able to insert two fingers between the front of the nose and the band itself. Also make sure that the browband is not too tight and not touching the ears, and that the throatlash is buckled so that you are able to put four fingers between the neck and the loop of the lash. All this might sound rather a lot to cope with, but I can assure you that every point is necessary.

Always allow yourself plenty of time to tack up, otherwise you might make mistakes in your haste and have regrets later in the day. At this stage you might be thinking that I am keeping on at you; well, I am, because it means that you will learn to do things properly which will benefit your horse or pony. That, in fact, is the sole purpose of this book.

One of the most important points to remember with tack is that it needs cleaning regularly, not only to keep it nice and clean and supple, but also to check that the leather is not wearing and the stitching is all right. Failure to look after your tack is not only dangerous and very stupid but expensive as well.

Ideally, you need a bridle hook and a saddle horse or rack when cleaning tack. But, if that is not possible, an alternative is to use an old, clean, folded linen tablecloth so that while you are cleaning the saddle the leather is not damaged. It is not as good as a saddle rack, of course, but when you have to watch the pennies, sometimes, you have to improvise, and in this instance a tablecloth will most certainly suffice. It must be washed regularly itself, or you will find flecks of cloth sticking to the leather.

You will need a sponge and a bar of glycerine saddle soap, which is easily obtained at a saddlers and is not expensive, and a bucket of tepid (never hot) water. Take the bridle to bits by undoing all the buckles and lay out the various pieces somewhere clean. Using a well wrung out sponge, clean each piece, ensuring that grease on the inside of the leather is removed. Change the water, wring out the sponge as much as possible and rub it on the saddle soap. Apply the soap to the bridle, rubbing in well, particularly the underside of the leather which is more absorbent. But remember, if you get a lather, the sponge is too wet.

It must be stressed that as leather 'breathes' and is 'fed' (by saddle soap) through its underside, it is essential to soap this area as well as the side which shows.

To remove the soap from the buckle holes poke them through with a deadened matchstick, or similar piece of wood. During the cleaning, which should be done every time you use your tack, make sure that you check all the stitching. If it is worn, get it put right at once. Never take chances because it just does not pay.

The bit should be washed, dried properly and then polished with a clean cloth. Some people recommend the use of metal polish on the bit but not me. I think that you can get the metal just as clean without it, particularly when it is cleaned daily. Just use a lot of elbow grease. It is different with the stirrup irons because, obviously, they are not going into the horse's mouth – or at least they should not be!

The bridle should be taken apart regularly so it is as well to know off by heart where everything fits. Once learned you will never forget it.

When you have finished with the bridle, hang it up on its peg by the headband, loop the reins over the top and give it a final sponging. Then wash your hands and set to work on the saddle.

Strip the saddle by taking off the girth and the stirrup leathers (removing the irons). As with the bridle, you must remove any dirt from the leather by using a well wrung-out sponge and going all over the saddle with it. Do not slosh gallons of water over it otherwise you will be in trouble, as the leather will eventually crack.

Then apply saddle soap to the saddle and to the leathers as well. Do not forget to wash and put soap on to the girth straps and flaps. Wash and dry the stirrup irons and then clean them up with metal polish. Now it is time to get to work on the girth. If it is nylon, webbing or string, wash with a pure soapy solution, rinse properly and allow to dry.

If the girth is made of leather, sponge off mud, remove

grease and then use saddle soap. The metal buckles must also be polished.

If your horse wears a numnah (saddle pad) which is made of imitation sheepskin or cotton, it must be cleaned of sweat and dirt and can then be put in the washing machine. Be sure, however, that you have your mother's approval first, and dry it thoroughly afterwards.

If you have a stable-kept pony who is clipped out during the winter, you will need a variety of rugs, including a jute rug, one or two blankets to go under the rug, depending on the weather, a day rug and also a New Zealand rug for use when he is turned out for periods during the day.

A jute rug is used as a night rug and has a woollen material lining to help keep the animal warm. It is held in place by a roller. The reason that you need a day rug as well as a night one is that the animal does not need to be kept as warm during the day, the temperature being higher, and a day rug is made of lighter material.

A New Zealand rug is made of canvas which is all-weather proof and is lined with a woollen material. It is worn in the field by stabled ponies and fine-coated grass-kept ponies in the winter. It is *never* worn in the stable, and must not be left on when wet.

After the New Zealand rug has been used for some time, the weather usually takes its toll and you will find that by the summer it needs re-proofing. This is a simple, if tedious, job which must be done unless you want the expense of buying another. Lay out the New Zealand rug on a clean surface (out of doors!) and wash the outside with soapy solution (not detergent) and a stiff brush. Turn the rug over and clean the inside, being careful not to damage the lining with the brush. When the rug has dried, probably several days later, apply the re-proofing liquid (available at camping shops) by painting it on with an old, clean brush. The liquid is the same as that used for re-proofing tents and is excellent. It is best to leave the rug indoors, over something (for example a step ladder) while it dries. Again, your parents' permission must be sought.

Apart from the winter rugs, there are also cotton summer

sheets, used to keep ponies clean in trailers or boxes on their way to shows, and anti-sweat rugs which are open mesh. These are used to dry off hot ponies without allowing them to catch cold, or to thatch wet ponies in the winter. Both are easily washed and dried in the washing machine.

During the summer, when the winter rugs are not being used, they should be mended and stored away for the next cold season.

In this chapter about tack, I also want to include the use of bandages for both legs and tail. If and when you use bandages, you must know how to put them on, otherwise they could damage the horse's or pony's tendons.

Exercise bandages are usually made of stockinette or crêpe. They are put on just below the knee to just above the fetlock joint and are secured with tapes which are tied on the outside of the leg (never on the inside) and tucked into the bandage. To help protect the actual leg, gamgee or special pads are placed around the area before the bandages are put on. It does, however, take practice to get the bandages on so that they remain in place. The idea is to give the legs extra support during exercise but do not try to use them without first taking expert advice.

Those bandages which are used to protect the horse in the stable, and to keep him warm in winter, go on just below the hocks and knees but also cover the fetlock. Only very thin skinned stabled horses need the extra warmth that stable bandages provide.

Tail bandages should only be used when travelling to shows. They are normally put on to dry tails to prevent injury or rubbing, and should not, contrary to popular belief, be used on wet or damp tails, because as the bandage dries it tightens and this restricts circulation.

At one stage the British Horse Society even sent out a circular to its members, telling them that it had been brought to their notice that some horses had suffered serious discomfort, because elasticated tail bandages used on wet tails had been left on too long.

You must remember to take the tail bandages off as quickly as possible.

Nowadays nearly all bandages are machine washable but remember that if you keep on pushing the elasticated ones in the tub, they tend to lose their elasticity.

When the bandages have been finished with, and washed, they should be rolled up and put away until you need to use them again.

One final word about bandages. Before you put them on you must check that there are no foreign objects clinging to the material, because any dirt or grit will make the pony's legs sore.

8
What to wear

Immediately parents start to think about riding clothes their minds begin to wrestle with the worrying thought of spending hundreds of pounds and the answer to many children is, 'No, we can't afford it.' That is certainly true nowadays. Still, if our politicians are to be believed, and I sincerely hope they are, we are slowly climbing back to the good times and will, one hopes, have some money to spend.

When you first start riding, however, it is silly to go out and spend a lot of money on jodhpurs, boots, jackets and so on until you are absolutely sure that you are really keen and want to ride for a long time to come. You can imagine what your parents would say if they invested a lot of their hard-earned money on a pair of jodhpurs and after six weeks you turned round and said, 'Well, I don't think I can be bothered to go riding any more.' It would be a complete financial waste and they would, rightly, be very angry with you. During your formative years there will be many hobbies you will want to try before settling to one which you truly love and which gives you great pleasure.

The most important item, and one which you *must* have at all times when you are riding, is a correct hat. It must have the Kite mark (a seal of approved safety) inside and it must also fit properly. A badly fitting hat is dangerous because if you ever fall off, it could not possibly offer you the protection for which it was designed. When first trying on a hat, put it firmly onto your head, fasten the chin-strap and shake your head up and down. If it feels comfortable, and does not

Always buy the right size hat

move, then the hat is a good fit. Never ride without a hat even for only a short time – it is not worth taking the risk.

Too many times I have seen young girls riding around the roads with their hair flowing in the wind trying, I suppose, to attract attention. It is a ridiculous thing to do and highly dangerous. If all you are concerned with is your beautiful image when you are on a pony, then you should not be riding. The best thing for you is a modelling job, and preferably one that does not involve the use of horses or ponies!

If you want to wear your hair long that is perfectly all right, but make sure that it properly covered with a riding hat when you are sitting on your horse. Some riding schools hire out hats to their clients, but often these are not in peak condition and cannot offer you full protection. They do not always fit properly either.

When first buying riding clothes, many people really do not know what size they are and for me, or anyone else, just to recommend that you acquire a hat that fits, without giving you a guide, is flippant. This chart will provide you with a fair idea of the measurements you may need.

Hat size chart

Hat size	6⅛	6¼	6⅜	6½	6⅝	6¾	6⅞	7	7⅛
Head measurement (inches)	19⅝	20⅛	20½	20⅞	21¼	21⅝	22	22½	22⅞
Head measurement (centimetres)	50	51	52	53	54	55	56	57	58

Before you go to a shop to buy a hat, first measure your head. Have someone put the tape around your skull so that it is in the middle of your forehead, and then make a note of the measurement. When you arrive at the shop, the assistant there will also measure you. If their measurement does not correspond with yours, find out why. If you measure too high on your forehead the hat will be too tight, and if you measure too low, you could end up with it falling over your eyes. Either way the hat will be unsatisfactory and unsafe.

One point to remember about hats is that if you ever damage one when falling off, you must buy a replacement at once. The reason for this is that the actual structure of it may have been affected because of the knock it has taken and, if that is the case, then you must change it for safety's sake. It may not feel any different but, believe me, if there is even a hairline crack in the superstructure then you mustn't take any chances.

Apart from having a good hat, you can also buy a safety strap that goes with it, so that if you do take a tumble the hat should not leave your head. Some are also designed to snap open if your head gets caught in the branches of a tree to prevent you throttling yourself. This type of chin-strap is certainly better than the ordinary, elasticated one, because under normal circumstances it will keep the hat firmly in place. In the past I have received a few letters from readers telling me that their hats have fallen off when they have had falls and although I fully sympathize with them, and were glad that they were not hurt, if they had bought the safety strap with their hats that would not have happened. I would also question whether their hats fitted properly in the first place.

As well as a proper hat you will also need a pair of jodhpur boots which have been designed with comfort in mind, as well as safety. When you place them into the stirrup irons they will not go straight through or get wedged unless, of course, you have the wrong sized irons attached to the leathers, a point I have already touched upon in the saddlery section. Do not, under any circumstances, wear high heels or platform shoes when you are riding because they can be dangerous. They also look absolutely ridiculous and show that you know nothing about riding and would be more at

High heels are dangerous!

home prancing around to the machinations of a pop group, in the safety of your own living room!

If you cannot afford to buy proper jodhpur boots, then the rubber riding type will do because they have been made with stirrup irons in mind. They are put together so well nowadays that, at first glance, it is difficult to actually tell that they are rubber. They are well-shaped and, in many cases, fit perfectly. All I would say is that if you suffer from hot feet (and many people do) then rubber might not suit your individual needs and you will have to save up for leather jodhpur boots. But, for the majority of riders, the rubber ones are ideal and, as far as cost goes, quite inexpensive.

I have only found one drawback with them as far as children are concerned and that is if they use the doorstep as a bootjack to remove them when they have finished riding. This can sometimes damage the heel and may eventually split the rubber. That is not the manufacturer's problem and the fault must lie with those who pull off their boots in this manner. A proper wooden bootjack does not cost a lot of money, can be kept in the garage if necessary and is an ideal way of taking your boots off without tearing them or damaging them in any way. But those who continue to hammer their heels up against the step will find riding very expensive indeed!

The good thing about rubber riding boots, if they happen to suit your feet, is that they can double as a wellington-type boot as well, and are completely waterproof. And, if they are properly looked after, you will also find that they do not immediately lose their shine.

The thing to do when you return home from a ride, or from work in the stables, is to wash off any mud, allow the boots to dry and then, as my own children do, spray them with furniture polish to keep them shiny. It is just a tip you might find helpful and does not cost a lot to implement. With all these things, however, it is just a question of the time you want or are able to devote to looking after your belongings. Always remember that if things are looked after they will last longer and, therefore, you will not be spending as much money on replacements.

Anyway, I never like to see young people riding their horses or ponies when dressed in shabby clothes and dirty boots. If they cannot be bothered to look after themselves, how on earth can they be trusted to look after a living creature? So, before you go to bed in the evening, make sure that you have cleaned your boots ready for the next riding session and never put it off until the morning – you will not want to do it then either and will use the excuse that you have not got time.

Once you have decided that riding is most certainly for you and that you will be in the saddle for a long time to come, you can start to think about buying a pair of jodhpurs, which are cut to make you as comfortable as possible on a horse or pony. The tight fit helps to keep the material in place so that it does not hurt your legs in any way. As a young man, I can remember not being given any good advice in this direction and, instead of saving up for a pair of jodhpurs, I would ride in an old pair of jeans or trousers. The result was that in winter my legs looked as though they had been rubbed for several hours with sandpaper, and when the wind was really biting I suffered from badly chapped legs. When my parents bought me a pair of jodhpurs my sore legs cleared up and I never suffered in that way again.

Jodhpurs are worth every penny you pay for them and, like any other riding equipment, should be looked after.

If you cannot afford to buy a pair and have to ride in jeans, do not wear skin-tight ones otherwise you will have difficulty mounting. You could find that they split which, apart from being embarrassing, is also very expensive.

There are some lovely jodhpurs on the market, including the stretch-type ones which are not only attractive but practical as well. On several occasions during past years I have run competitions in the *Daily Mail* Pony Club column which have been staged with the generous help of the Caldene Clothing Company from Yorkshire. That company supplied the prizes of 'Cavalier' jodhpurs which were much appreciated by young readers throughout Britain. Carl Uttley, a director of the firm, has spent a lot of his time travelling the world looking for value to give youngsters who

are interested in riding. He knows, like many other manufacturers and wholesalers, that the customer must be given a
good deal and he, and they, make sure that you get it.

'We spent two years designing and testing the "Cavalier"
before ever putting them on the market,' said Mr Uttley.
'And when we did, they were a great success, I am happy to
say.'

What advice would a man of his experience give to the
young person who is going to buy a pair of jodhpurs for the
first time and is, naturally, unsure of what to look for or,
indeed, what sort to buy?

'Always go to a local stockist and be advised by them,
because they have probably had many years of experience
and will be able to help with the size and quality of the
produce. The best shops to go to are those which are well
stocked, because the choice will obviously be greater. I
would also advise that they buy a proprietary brand of
garment, because they will have been made by people who
have had experience and knowledge of jodhpur manufactur-
ing. Most jodhpurs that are sold nowadays for the mass
market come in three sizes – short, regular and long. With
the advent of modern fabrics the well-fitting jodhpur should,
in fact, look like a second skin.'

If you do not know the name of a stockist in your area,
write to Mr Uttley at Caldene Clothing Company,
Mytholmroyd, Hebdon Bridge, Yorkshire, enclosing a self-
addressed, stamped envelope and he will send you the names
of shops in your area.

'We have lists of stockists, prepared by county, so that if
someone wrote to me say, from Buckinghamshire, I would
send them the list of shops in that area, even if they do not
sell Caldene clothing. We all want to give the public as much
help as we can because we happen to think that is important.'

Incidentally, it is worth remembering that coloured jodhpurs do not show the dirt as much as plain ones.

When you are first starting to ride there is no need to
spend a lot of money on a new hacking jacket because that,
too, can be expensive if there is a chance that you will be

giving up riding after a short while. The best thing to do is to look on the stable notice board at the local riding school and see if you can purchase a second-hand one.

Children grow out of garments with amazing rapidity and it is not wise just to throw something out because it does not fit anymore. There is always someone, somewhere, who could make use of a discarded riding jacket and, fortunately, mothers whose children like horses have a good habit of selling off clothes they can no longer use. Most stables have a board in the office with items for sale and it is sensible to look and buy if necessary.

If you cannot afford to wear a proper hacking jacket (and you will really only need one for shows or rallies) then to start with there is no harm in putting on an anorak or zip up windcheater. But riding clothes have been designed with a specific job in mind and are always that much better. It does, however, depend very much on how much money you can afford to spend.

Apart from the articles of clothing I have already mentioned, you will also need a pair of gloves, preferably string-type ones, which are ideal for ordinary everyday hacking. Do not wear mittens, because you will find you cannot hold the reins properly and are not, therefore, in full control of your pony. Leather gloves are all very well for showing, but would not last long with the heavy work you would subject them to if you wore them every day. I also find that if I am riding a horse that is strong and I am wearing leather gloves, the reins tend to slip through my fingers when sweat gets on the leather. That is why I like to ride with rubber reinforced reins, because they help to alleviate that problem and allow me to get a good grip when it is raining. Having said that, though, I do know that some youngsters do not like rubber-backed reins because they are too thick to hold between their fingers. If you find the same thing, then you are far better off with standard leather reins because, apart from being safe when you are riding, you also need to be comfortable.

Riding in very wet weather can be frustrating and it is wise to have a spare set of ordinary clothes with you to change into afterwards. The two main reasons for this are that (a) you do not want to catch a cold and (b) it is uncomfortable to walk around when feeling like a drowned rat. If the heavens have opened before your ride and you want to attempt to keep dry, then put on a pair of waterproof trousers over your jodhpurs. They can easily be bought from your local camping shop and are not at all expensive. There is one drawback, however. Although some of them keep you perfectly dry from the waist to shin-bone, they then drip water slowly and surely into your jodhpur boots. That is why it is advantageous to wear rubber riding boots with over-trousers. If you cannot afford to buy a proper rainproofed mac (and they are very good) then for ordinary use try a cagoule which is a lot cheaper and will keep you dry but will not, of course, last you as long.

If you do get a good soaking and do not have any spare clothes handy, make sure your pony is comfortable, then go home, have a bath and change your clothes. The obvious reason for telling you to dry your pony first is that he cannot do it himself. If he is hot and wet, and you leave him to fend for himself, he could develop a chill.

It is now time to tell you about shows and what you should wear if you decide to take part in them. I will assume that you can already ride properly and that you want to have fun going round the local shows in the hope of winning yourself a few rosettes and, even if you do not, having a good time, anyway.

You will need a hacking jacket because the judges, even at a very local level, do not like to see people competing in multi-colours or in bomber-type jackets which make you look more like a fighter-pilot than a rider. And they are correct to think like that, because when you go to a show you should want to look smart and to wear the proper clothes. Apart from the jacket, you will also need jodhpur boots, gloves and, of course, a good pair of jodhpurs. Some people might say that you should have breeches and long boots, but at the level I am talking about they are not necessary. You would, I hope, be a member of the Pony Club and should be wearing the standard tie, secured by a tie-pin.

If you are over sixteen, however, you can wear long rubber riding boots for riding and show classes, as short boots tend to look rather peculiar on long legs! This also works out well as far as economy goes, because the older you are, the bigger your feet are and the more expensive the jodhpur boots become. And many young ladies think that they are rather ungainly.

For competing in Pony Club hunter trials a hacking jacket, a good pair of gloves, jodhpurs and boots are ideal. If you are chosen to compete in a Pony Club inter-branch hunter trials, then usually the special equipment, like number cloth and 'colours', will be provided for you by your branch. If, when you are older, you are lucky enough to take part in hunter trials at national level, you would have to make or buy your own 'colours'; or if you have the time and the ability, you could knit them yourselves.

In racing, colours are used to identify the horse and its owner, but in hunter trials the bright colours used are not for that at all. One good reason for them is that if a rider falls out in the country and is injured, he is easily found (or usually so) by ambulance men and women. And, having attended many trials, I can testify to the colours' usefulness in this particular respect. If you are injured the quicker you are taken to hospital the better, so being found quickly is essential.

Many young people have taken to riding dressage which is a lovely sport. If we could ever be as expert at it as the West Germans then I, for one, would be a very happy man. We do have a long way to go to achieve that but as long as youngsters are interested they should be given every encouragement. It is also a good pastime for a pony and rider who are not over-keen on jumping. It exercises the brain, as well as the body, and is a super family sport – by that I mean mother, father and children can all go and watch and have a lovely day out.

If you are riding, you can do so in a hacking jacket or a black show jacket. This means, however, that you will probably have to buy the latter and only wear it at dressage shows. That is an expensive thing to do. So my advice is to stick to the ever faithful multi-purpose hacking jacket for Pony Club dressage. If you reach a high standard and maybe represent Britain at national, or, indeed, international level, you would be required to wear long black leather boots, white breeches, a black tailed jacket and top hat. That is rather superior and for most of you, alas, out of reach. Grand Prix-type dressage is very hard and only the very best and utterly dedicated horses and riders ever reach the top. There is, however, no earthly reason why you should not set your sights high and aim for the top. I merely point out that you will have a long, hard slog to get there.

Most of you will only be concerned with competition at a much more local level but, like the experts, you will still have to look after the clothes you have. Whenever you use your hacking jacket brush the hairs from it when you return home, then hang it in the wardrobe covered with a polythene bag.

9
Joining the Pony Club and road safety

For anyone who has a pony, or is very interested in riding, joining the British Horse Society's Pony Club is a must. It offers practically everything a young person wants in the way of education, fun and relaxation and is also a wonderful opportunity to meet other people with the same interests and feelings for ponies. You can join the Pony Club up to the age of seventeen and, after that, you become an Associate member until you reach the age of twenty-one. At the time of writing, enrolment costs just 50p and the annual subscription is a mere £7.

The organization, which has proved a great success, has over 100,000 members around the world and even has branches in Saudi Arabia, Thailand, Kenya, Malaysia and the Philippines. In Britain all you have to do to join is approach your local District Commissioner and ask for the appropriate forms. Anyone at a nearby riding school will know who the Commissioner is and will probably tell you how to contact her. If they cannot, then write to the Secretary of the Pony Club, whose head office is at the British Equestrian Centre, Stoneleigh, Warwickshire, and ask her.

Apart from all the tests you can take and lectures you may attend, there will also be rallies and camps you will be able to go to which are run in the school holidays. They are great fun and will not only teach you a lot about horses and ponies, but also a lot about yourself as well. The Executive Officer of the Pony Club is a man called Lt Colonel Bill Lithgow, who has had a wealth of experience dealing with young people as well as international competitors. In fact, he used to be a well-known three-day event rider himself and so is a person who well knows what he is talking about and in what direction the Pony Club is going.

If you are wondering if there is a Pony Club branch near you, I would be almost certain that there is because there are 360 in the United Kingdom and 1,344 branches in twenty-five countries overseas. That shows just how popular it is here and abroad.

Once you have joined you will need certain specific clothing, which does not have to be purchased all at once, and which will, of course, include jodhpurs, jacket, riding hat and jodhpur boots or long rubber boots. The Club recommends that you should not wear plimsolls or wellingtons in the interests of safety because, as I have explained in an earlier chapter, your feet could slide through the stirrup irons and lead to you being dragged. They also insist that even if your clothes are not new they are clean and tidy. You must look presentable.

When you become a member you will have the opportunity of being taught to the standard of the proficiency tests A, H, B, C and D. A is the highest qualification in this section and D, being the lowest, is of course the first one you will be required to take. Even if you are not too clever at school, you will be amazed what your brain will soak up when you are totally interested in a subject, particularly if that subject happens to be horses and ponies. Anyone who belongs to the Pony Club is expected to enter for the tests.

One of the very useful bonuses of becoming an Associate member or member of the Pony Club, is that you are automatically insured against third party legal liability arising from equestrian activities, up to the mammoth amount of £250,000. This safeguards you for any injury or damage caused by your pony to another person or their property. That is a very good insurance and one that is well worth having, because no matter how safe your pony is on the roads, or anywhere else, accidents can happen. If you

Don't hog the road

have the correct insurance it can take a lot of worry from your mind.

There are other very good insurances you can take out, particularly with the Norwich Union, but the one mentioned above is incorporated in the money you pay for your annual Pony Club subscription. The business is, therefore, taken care of before you even realize that you need to be insured for any third party legal liability. I suppose that the Club finds that with so many members it can get a fair deal at a reasonable premium and that is what you want. I also know from personal experience that the people at the Norwich Union will give you good value for your money.

Apart from the tests already mentioned there is another and, in my opinion, vital proficiency exam called the Riding and Road Safety Certificate. The aim of this particular exam is to point out the dangers of riding on the roads of Britain, and to tell you how to cope with them so that neither you nor your pony gets hurt. I say that this test is very important because not many of you will realize that by the time you go to bed every night there have been eight accidents on the roads involving horses and ponies. And, although the blame must be shared equally between drivers and riders, they are statistics which should be registered in the recesses of the mind and remembered when you are riding on the roads.

Although I have known of many people, young and old, who have failed this test because they did not know the correct way to ride or behave on roads, I congratulate them for even taking the exam because it shows they were interested enough to bother. I am happy to add that when they took the exam for a second time most of them passed. The whole point about tests and examinations is that you must realize they have been devised by experts for your benefit. If you fail once, always try again and again until you pass. It is easy to think you cannot do something, simply because you find it hard – but if you can overcome nerves, or a bad memory, then you have every justification for feeling proud of yourself. And, even if you do not realize it, you will be doing your pony a favour, too, and making his life that much safer.

If you have to ride on the roads, and in the suburbs it is very difficult not to, remember that you should travel on the left of the road when mounted. If you are leading a horse or pony you should do that from the left-hand side, keeping yourself between the traffic and the animal. Never assume, either, that drivers know what you intend to do. Many of them do not understand horses, or realize how easily they are frightened, and that can be bad news for you.

To be safe, always think that the person who is driving needs help. When you want to turn off the road, say on to a minor section or bridleway, make sure that you allow yourself plenty of time and give very clear, sure signals so that the person behind the wheel would have to be blind-folded or stupid not to see what you were doing.

If you are riding on the roads with other people, do not ride abreast but in single file, with the safest pony leading the way. Do not ever spread across the road like a bunch of cowboys looking for stray cows. If you do, you are asking for trouble in the form of an accident. Many people even ride two abreast, talking, and assume that everyone else knows what they are doing. The authorities say that two abreast is all right, but I do not like it, particularly on busy roads. I know some people will say, 'Well, supposing there is a young, inexperienced horse on the roads, he will need something on his outside to help keep him calm.' My answer to that is that the nervous horse or pony should not be on a busy road in the first place and until he has gained road experience on quiet roads and lanes, he should not go anywhere near busy roads. Do not be clever where horses and ponies are concerned – just play it safe for their sake and yours.

If you need to talk when you are walking or trotting your mount along the road do so, but from behind – there is no need at all to ride two abreast when there is a lot of traffic in the vicinity. If you do eventually have to take a young horse on the roads, always wear a tabard which clearly states 'Caution – Young Horse' or words to that effect. Do not be proud on these occasions and feel that having a coloured piece of material across your back does not suit you. That, if you think about it, is not the object of the exercise. And when good drivers slow down and give you a wide berth, have the decency to thank them for their efforts so that they get something out of it, too. If you behave like a fool, you must expect to be treated like one.

Courtesy does not cost anyone anything, but it most certainly goes a long way with drivers. Travelling through Gloucestershire I happened to drive down a country lane where several very young people were riding ponies and, as I went very slowly past, each one of the children thanked me. They were being looked after by an elderly lady and if she is reading this book I want to thank her from the bottom of my heart. Those youngsters will always be safe on the roads and so will their ponies, because they were taught properly.

Another point to be aware of is that if you are riding on the road during the early evening, you should wear orange tabards and stirrup lights, available from Stoneleigh, so that drivers can see you from some way off and avoid running into your pony. If you can avoid it, however, stay off the roads at night and also, I might add, when they are snowy or icy in the winter. They can be terribly dangerous then.

It is easy to see why the Pony Club is such an important organization as far as young people are concerned, and why it should be supported in every practical way. Those who run the Club are experts with only your interests and those of your ponies at heart. When I looked back at my records, it was interesting to note that many of our Olympic gold medal winners for three-day eventing started their careers in the Pony Club, and look what it helped them to achieve!

The District Commissioner of your Pony Club will also organize rallies which can be great fun for all the family. It sometimes means that mothers work twice as hard as they normally do but, if they are anything like my wife, they also enjoy watching you being happy and having a lot of fun with your ponies. Parents sometimes get roped in to help out, and that is not at all a bad thing because none of the equestrian disciplines or organizations could exist in the form that they do today without voluntary help from keen adults. I must also tell you that, if you do join the Pony Club, you will be

Living well at Wembley

expected to support the working rallies of your particular
branch. Failure to do so can result in your membership being
terminated.

At all the rallies throughout the land there is usually
instruction given in saddlery, equitation and management of
the pony. These instructional activites are also accompanied
by mounted games and sports. And, for those of you who are
not lucky enough to own your own pony, dismounted rallies
are held for your benefit. This means everyone has the
opportunity to take part.

Early every year most Pony Club branches go into training for the Mounted Games Championship, the final of
which is held every October at the Horse of the Year Show in
Wembley. In this particular competition, devised I might
add, with you in mind, there are regional finals and zone
finals and the lucky few who succeed go on to Wembley
where they live in caravans in the complex and, it seems, eat
their way through mountains of baked beans and fish and

chips! Competition is hot, though, and if a team does get through the qualifiers, and then to the final, they have done very well indeed.

The Prince Philip Cup, for the Pony Club Mounted Games Championship, is sponsored by the *Daily Mail* and Butlins and is organized by the British Horse Society. The man who has looked after this event at Wembley for many years now is famous equestrian commentator Raymond Brooks-Ward, fondly known to those who take part as 'Uncle Raymond'. He works very hard in seeing that everything runs smoothly and then excites onlookers so much during the games with his efficient commentary that they almost fall out of their chairs and into the arena! During that week at Wembley, Butlins put up the money to stage their own Pony Club competition as well. It is always a success and they are to be congratulated.

Being a member of your local branch gives you the opportunity of taking part in such competitions, and it is the only chance most of you will ever get of actually riding at this highly popular venue, along with such world famous names as David Broome, Harvey Smith, Malcolm Pyrah and Caroline Bradley, who compete in the show jumping there at the same time.

The Prince Philip Cup gives you the opportunity to show courage, determination and all-round riding ability. Sometimes, at the Wembley show, the youngsters leave the arena so fast it seems they will never pull up outside, fortunately they always do, somehow. To ride in these games you must be under 15 years of age and the pony you ride must be at least four years old, and may not exceed 14.2 hands high. There are other rules, too, which include the one that if you are over 8 stones 5 pounds you may not partner a pony which is 12.2 hands high or under. Each branch of the Pony Club may enter a team, but must also pay a fee. After the area qualifiers there are zone finals and the winning team from each of the zone competitions goes through to the final at Wembley. Those who triumph in the final are all given a medal to celebrate the occasion.

The whole thing is extremely well organized and for the

area qualifiers and zone finals, grants at the rate of 15 pence per mile (return journey) are paid to teams for each mile they have to travel over 100 miles. If a team's journey to the games exceeds 300 miles, it may claim £12.50, over 600 miles £25, and over 900 miles £37. The money is paid by the Pony Club after expenses have been submitted. At the final of the Championship a grant is also given to the teams towards travelling and living expenses and the ponies are stabled free. Seats at the show are provided for the members of the teams plus two adults from each team. The expenses mentioned are correct at the time of writing, but could fluctuate with inflation. For those of you who are interested in riding for your branch of the Pony Club, the games you will have to train for in the area qualifiers are team bending relay, the mug race, tyre race, bottle race, groom's stakes and litter race. There is also a spare competition which is called the postman's chase.

At the zone finals, there will be team bending, groom's stakes, sword race, Windsor game, stepping-stone dash, bottle race, litter race, Butlin Hi-Lo game, the tyre race and the five flag race – you have to take part in all these competitions mounted, of course. A team trainer from your local branch will be there at all times to guide you in the right direction and, it is to be hoped, eventually to Wembley's Horse of the Year show.

I will not describe what you have to do in each game because by the time you read this chapter the organizers may well have changed the format. I mention the above to give you a guide as to what you can expect.

Apart from the branches organizing entries into the Prince Philip Cup, the Pony Club officials (and I might add a lot of unpaid helpers) also lay on films and lectures for their members and these are not only highly educational but great fun as well. Anyone who has ever attended a lecture given by that great show jumping rider Harvey Smith will know exactly what I mean. Riders, trainers and officials from all the disciplines take part in the lectures to do their bit for youngsters of the Pony Club. They know what it is like to be hungry for knowledge and they go out of their way to help.

During the summer school holidays youngsters are also invited by their branch secretary, or District Commissioner, to go on a week's camping holiday with their ponies. This can be an ideal way for you to get used to being away from your parents for a short while under the best and most caring supervision. While you are at camp, usually on a farmer's land, you will live in tents and your ponies will live out. You will play mounted games, go on visits and, if you are near the beach, you will be able to take your ponies along the sealine so that they can dip their legs in and splash about. It is all very safe and a good time is had by all who go on such holidays. At the end of the short camp the organizers sometimes lay on a gymkhana to which all parents are invited for the day.

As you have to look after yourselves during the time you are there, it provides good training for you, among friends for the future. It also helps to make you think for yourselves and solve your own problems.

There is always someone on hand if you get into real difficulties, but everything normally runs like clockwork and you will have a really good time. Usually there are adult helpers in the camp who cope with the cooking, so that you do not run the risk of burning yourself – or going hungry. Those who plan the trips do a fine job, which is much appreciated by all.

Apart from camps, the Prince Philip Cup, and other such activities, the Pony Club also organize inter-branch events, which include a polo tournament, a tetrathlon championship and a show jumping championship. Although some of you might think that polo is a game played only by the very wealthy, nothing is further from the truth, although rich people do play of course. The game is gaining in popularity and many youngsters in the Pony Club take part in matches held all over the country, with sponsors like Texaco stepping in and helping out financially.

There is no reason, really, why many of you should not play polo. If you have a pony, there is not much more that you have to buy to be in a position to play. And, providing the pony is versatile, fit and healthy he should also enjoy the proceedings. Again, it is all well supervised, with expert instruction.

Some of you may also enjoy a visit to a stud, or hunting stable. That is all taken care of, too. Every so often each branch will organize such trips, and for a whole day you will enjoy seeing how the other half live. I once made a trip to Kentucky to have a look at the studs they have in the 'Blue Grass' country there and it is something that I have never forgotten. On that visit I saw some of the best and most expensive Thoroughbreds in the world, who are looked after like kings and queens. When you think about it, that is exactly what they are in their own equine world. Although you are unlikely to end up in America, a trip to an English stud can be very interesting.

Apart from being good fun, the trips are highly educational. Talking about learning, the Pony Club always has many publications on sale at Stoneleigh and anyone who is interested can write to the bookshop there and ask for a pamphlet of those books that are available. There is always a large stock and, if you wanted to, you could spend all of your free time reading about the animals you love so dearly.

I am a great believer in knowledge, because if you are able to fully understand a subject, most of the time you will be able to solve any problems that may arise, which is most important when dealing with horses and ponies. Too many people take them for granted and treat them like machines. The Pony Club, and the people who run it, are interested in helping everyone, because they know that the more information that is available to the public, the more chance there is of equines being looked after in the correct way.

They also know that if they can encourage you to join them at an early age you will get a lot more fun out of life and, they hope, grow up to be a responsible person, especially where animals are concerned.

In this day and age, many of you might not fully understand that philosophy but, you can take it from me, they know exactly what they are doing and only have your interests at heart.

If you study the list of Pony Club branches operating

throughout the world, you do not have to be a genius to realize that many young people are getting a lot of enjoyment out of being with horses and ponies. Occasionally some Pony Club branches in Britain are given the opportunity to visit their colleagues abroad. What better way is there of improving relations with those who live overseas?

10
Travelling and loading

When you go on a long train, bus or car journey you like to be comfortable and feel safe for every mile of the trip. So does a horse or pony. The easiest thing in the world is for the animal to become restless and it is up to you to prevent this and give him confidence. If he is badly frightened being loaded into the box, or while travelling in it, he will never forget the experience. Some horses behave superbly when they are in their stable but the moment they get anywhere near a horsebox ramp they start dancing all over the place as if auditioning for a part in Swan Lake. This is a time when you will need to exercise your mental powers of self-restraint. If you panic, or lose your temper, because your horse refuses to go up the ramp, nobody wins. The crucial test will probably come when time is short and several other things have already conspired to make you late – then, to end it all, your mount simply refuses to put one hoof in front of the other.

At that moment you will either start tearing your hair out, strand by strand, or be reduced to a jibbering idiot, giving up the battle and conceding defeat with unconditional surrender. I sympathize, of course, but if it is not too late, do not give in. Some people, when they have come up against an awkward loader, believe that they are stronger than the horse or pony and proceed to flex their muscles, blow hard through their teeth, and attempt to drag the animal up the ramp and into his compartment. Such tough guy stuff is out for three reasons: (1) the animal is stronger that you; (2) the headcollar will probably snap and he will canter off down the road causing havoc; and (3) you will frighten the living daylights out of him and he will never want to go anywhere near a horsebox or trailer again.

A man I know who did not care how the horse he was looking after went into the box as long as it did, paid dearly one day for abusing the gelding in his charge. After much thought with his pea-sized brain, he decided that pushing a bristled hard broom up beneath the animal's tail would have the desired effect of making him go forward. I am happy to relate that it did not and when the broom made contact the man on the other end was introduced rather rapidly to the hind shoes of the gelding. He was in hospital for a fortnight! Cruelty never pays, you see, even if it is practised in anger, frustration or plain stupidity, and those who resort to it will be sorry. You have to try and find your way into the mind of the horse in the quietest way possible. Once you have

Always remain cool, calm and collected when loading

discovered the reasons for his dislike of horseboxes or
trailers, you can then help him, and yourself – it is, I
suppose, psychology out of the saddle.

And the only way to begin is to give yourself plenty of time
because, if you do not, you cannot practise what I call the
'gentle method of persuasion'. This involves a lot of talk and
neck stroking and, although the diehards might not agree, it
will work if you allow it to. Firstly, if the animal is hesitant
when being loaded, and you know it, walk him up to the box
or trailer as if you have got all day and are not really
interested in whether he goes in or not. The reason for doing
this is that if you start to get angry, upset or worried, those
feelings will be transmitted to him. But if he thinks you are
calm, in control and are not being unkind, you will have
more chance of success. It is vital that the floor of the
horsebox or trailer is adequately covered with straw as this
will prevent the pony slipping (something which will really
frighten him). It is also a good idea to spread some straw on
the ramp as well.

Always persevere. Never get angry or tense and, whatever
you do, do not hit him. If he goes halfway up the ramp and
then stops, allow him some time, pat him on the neck and
keep talking to him all the time. In your pocket somewhere
you might even have a small cube of sugar and, after telling
him what a clever chap he has been to have got so far up
such a horribly steep ramp, give him the sugar and try to get
him to go the rest of the way.

If he is clever, he will eat the sugar and stay exactly where
he is, either hoping you will give him another lump or to test
your willpower. Ponies, in particular, usually know all the
moves and that is why you have got to be clever enough to
beat them at their own game. You can only do that by
thinking deeper than they do, and encouraging them to
believe that they are winning, when, in fact, you are. If your
pony does stop midway up the ramp, talk or sing to him and
run your right hand down his nearside leg so that he will
think you are going to pick up his foot to look at his shoe
(remember you will be leading him into the box or trailer
from the left-hand side). When you have had a look at the

shoe, try to persuade him to put his foot down further than it was before. Then, without looking at him, try and lead him up into the box. Just for your information, you should never try to outstare animals, or peer into their eyes for any length of time. They don't like it very much and it tends to unsettle them.

If this method fails to get him where he should be, and again I insist you give him ample time, put down more straw on the ramp to cut down any noise and make the whole thing more acceptable to him. It really is incredible how even the slightest creak as he goes to walk up the ramp can put him off the whole idea.

And, if you think about it, walking straight up into a large box on wheels must be very frightening anyway. That is why everything you do at this stage must be done gently and, above all, quietly.

All he should be hearing is your voice and any birds who may be singing! At least then you know he is calm and not about to take off backwards at great speed. Laying straw down in the ramp does tend to make a lot of mess in the yard, or on the road, but that is something you will have to put up with. As long as you sweep it all up afterwards nobody should mind in the least. If the straw does not do the trick, leave it down there and ask your friend to get some goodies from the food store. It may be that your pony is very keen on root vegetables, like carrots or parsnips – if he is then, holding the headcollar in your right hand, and still standing to the nearside, dangle one of them in front of him and move up with him so that the vegetable is always just out of mouthwatering reach. I do not normally like offering bribes to animals, but in the case of loading them into a horsebox or trailer, I do feel fully justified in resorting to it.

If you still have not reached your goal, then it is time to bring up the reserves (your friends) with a lunge rein. While you are still trying to lead him in, they will hold either end of the lunge so that the centre of it rests on the animal's bottom. Then gently, very gently, they can walk towards the box whilst you, looking straight ahead, try to lead your pony up the ramp. Remember, as soon as the pony is in, the breeching strap (this goes behind his bottom) must be fastened speedily so that he cannot run back.

I am a great believer in giving horses and ponies plenty of time even if you are late and need to get a move on. When the animal first sees a new box let him have a long, hard look at it so that he can work himself up to being brave. Also, allow him to sniff at it so that he will realize it is not going to hurt him. If you are really clever, you will have laid a trail of oats leading into the horsebox. With any luck, he will devour them and, before he realizes what has happened, he will be safely ensconced. If that happens, make a fuss of him and give him a carrot (remember, cut lengthways).

To give yourself more chance of encouraging the horse or pony in, make sure your box is parked so that one part of the ramp is blocked off by a wall or hedge. This means that if he is the sort who likes to launch himself into space halfway up the ramp, there is only one side available for him to do it and you will have more chance of stopping him. Remember, too, that many horses and ponies are difficult to load simply because the interior of the box or trailer is dark and looks frightening. Avoid parking the vehicle in shadow and before loading switch on any interior lights so that the animal can see where he is going. Once he is in, tie him up on a shortish headcollar rope attached to the appropriate ring at the front of the box. Horses, I have found, travel best when they are facing the front and can look at the person in charge of them. Remember that you have to use a quick-release knot for safety.

In the bad old days some people used to travel their horses loose, but that is dangerous and should not be practised. Many years ago I knew of a racehorse who would not travel any other way and when the box set off for the races the gelding would just lie down and go to sleep. But he was unique and you should not let your horse follow suit.

Because your mount is travelling in a box, he will need to be fully protected from any knocks he might take along the way if the driver has to brake to avoid an accident or merely takes a corner too sharply. That should never happen but it is best to play safe. Experienced horsebox drivers are among the best in the business and know that the animals in their charge rely totally on them for a smooth and safe ride. They will go out of their way to ensure that the horses have an easy time when travelling.

If you are making your journey during the winter your horse or pony will need to have a rug on to keep him warm. Because he is standing in a confined space, he will not be able to stimulate his circulation and, therefore, you must help him out with a rug. In summer, when the weather is much more to everyone's liking, a sweat sheet is all he will need. There are, however, several important items all horses must wear when travelling: a tail guard, leg protectors, bandages and hock boots. Once they are on, he will not come to much harm and you will know in your own mind that there is nothing else you can to do make him safe. If your horse has to travel a fairly long distance, make sure you feed him before he leaves and give him water. Also ensure he has a haynet full of hay to munch on the trip. This will prevent hunger pangs and will go a long way to making him happy

keep him warm in winter

and content. I would also recommend that, if the journey is very long, you allow him to stretch his legs halfway there so that he does not stiffen up. It will also give him access to fresh air, which we all need to keep going.

If your journey is more than, say, six hours, I would also suggest that you split it in two, and arrange for your pony to spend a night in a stable somewhere. As far as I am concerned, his comfort comes first and if he associates happy times with travelling, you will never have any trouble getting him into a horsebox. Give him a hard time, however, and you could end up with a mental wreck on your hands – and nobody in their right minds would want that to happen.

Before you leave to go to a show, or on any other journey, you should make sure that you have some spare string with you to secure to the outside of the box, so that when you arrive at the show, or stop to give your horse or pony a chance to stretch his legs, you can tie his headcollar rope to it. If you are riding your mount at a show, it is not wise, or kind, to leave him in the horsebox all the time because he can get bored and, in the height of summer, very hot. In the summer, put the string on the side of the box which is casting a shadow and tie your mount to it. That will keep him out of the sun and he will be comfortable, providing he also has a drink of water and a small amount of hay to eat. Always think of his comfort.

Apart from your horse's personal safety, if you have a trailer it must also be checked regularly. Remember, too, that it is an offence to travel in it with your mount. You may go in a horsebox, because there is a groom's compartment built in for you, but travelling in a trailer is illegal. One of the first checks to be made is on the tyres because, if they are of different pressures, your mount could be in for an uncomfortable ride. Ask the driver, one of your parents or a senior member of your riding school to do this. A tyre pressure gauge is very cheap to buy and so there is no reason why you should not have one in your possession.

If the driver has not had the trailer long, it is a good idea for him or her to practise driving the car with the empty vehicle attached to it – this is so that he/she gets used to the width and length of the car and trailer. The driver must also remember to proceed very sympathetically when the horse or pony is in the back, otherwise he or she will frighten the animal and put him off travelling. Another important thing to be checked is the coupling which links the trailer to the car. It should be scrutinized when the parts are first married together and again before driving off. The trailer's stop-lights should also be checked, so that when the driver does have to pull up during the journey other drivers behind will know exactly what he or she aims to do.

The floor of the trailer must also be inspected regularly, for obvious reasons. If you are in any doubt at all a garage will be only too pleased to give it a thorough examination. You cannot be too careful when dealing with trailers and horseboxes and it is far better to double check than be wrong and sorry for it afterwards. The clips on the ramp are also very important. Check that they are done up properly before embarking on your journey.

Travelling to any destination is always hard work because there are usually a hundred and one things to remember to take. Most of the stuff can be piled into the back of the car but if everything has been rather hectic, and the horse has delayed you, you are apt to forget several items – usually the ones you can least afford to be without. The best thing to do is to make a list of everything you will need and, before loading your mount into the box, tick off each piece of equipment as you put it in the car. Always remember, too, to take a water container and rubber buckets in case there is no running water where you are going. Fill the container with fresh water and try to keep it in a cool place.

Take spares of everything, including stirrup leathers and reins, because there is nothing worse than making all the preparations, getting to a show, riding and then a leather breaking, forcing you to stop competing for the rest of the day. If you do not have a replacement, all of your organizing and hard work will have been for nothing. If you are at a show, try and park the horsebox or trailer in a shady spot, so that it is not like an oven when you get ready to return home. I know that is not always possible, but if you get there in plenty of time something can always be worked out.

Having made sure that your horse is comfortable, you should also make sure that you are, too, and that means taking a flask of coffee or tea with you and some sandwiches. At some shows such necessities are very expensive and, anyway, you might have to queue for ages trying to get them. So it is much wiser to make your own arrangements. When you have competed in your classes do not leave your pony tied up and sweating. Take him for a walk and allow him to settle down and cool off. Afterwards offer him water and give him a munch of hay.

When the show is over pack everything up again in a neat and tidy fashion. Your horse or pony will be tired and the last thing he wants is to be thrown all over the place on his way home, so the driver should take extra care. When you arrive at the stable, see that your horse or pony is bedded down for the night, fed and watered. Then take out and put away all the items you used at the show. If you are not too tired, it is a wise move to sponge over your bridle, and saddle, apply some saddle soap and allow it to soak in overnight. Sometimes, however, such things have to wait until the following day and if they do, do not forget to do them.

11
Ailments

To enjoy your horse or pony to the full means keeping him well and free from anything which might upset him mentally or physically. From your own experiences, you know that if you catch a cold, or something worse, your whole routine is thrown out and you might feel ghastly for some time. Horses are no different from you in this respect and when they have a runny nose, or feel a little off colour, the last thing they want you to do is gallop them off their feet. In this chapter I am going to deal with the ailments which may affect your mount and show you how to prevent some even gaining a hold at all.

One of the most common of complaints which you are bound to experience is equine influenza – I say bound to, because although it is common knowledge that epidemics sometimes sweep this country with a vengeance, too many people try to close the door when the trouble has already gained entrance. It is then too late to stop it affecting your horse and others with whom he comes into contact.

There are two basic strains of equine influenza and during the last twenty-one years there have been eight major outbreaks: in 1963 of type 1, in 1965 of type 2, 1969 of type 2, 1973 of type 1, 1976 of type 2, 1977 of type 1 and 1979 of type 2. I go into detail about the two types since they are very important. It was because of the various attacks by these two viruses that vaccination was initiated in the United Kingdom in 1969.

But although many people have been warned how dangerous equine influenza is, only one horse or pony in seven has been adequately protected against the viruses, and when you consider that there are some three-quarters of a million equines in Britain it is easy to see why the veterinary profession is concerned about the whole thing. These experts have done their best to point out the dangers and it is up to us to see that we look after the animals in our care, giving them the protection they should have against these dreadful viruses.

I do not intend to bore you with figures, or blind you with science, but I feel it is a good idea to give you the statistical records of vaccine administrations. In the ten years from 1970 to 1980, vaccinations actually rose from 21,000 to a total of 226,370. But a year later they dropped by a massive 207,230. Now there may be several reasons for this, including the fact that Britain was going through a bad time

If you think he's got flu, call the vet

economically and owners might have been cutting back on the things they did not think were important and at that particular time there was not an outbreak of equine influenza. It was, however, a dangerous situation because, if the virus had struck, with thousands of horses not protected it could have gained a hold which would have proved difficult to break.

The most interesting feature of all this is that outbreaks of flu seem to come after gaps of two to three years, and it is also interesting to note that when there was a major outbreak of A Equi 2 – not only in this country, but in Ireland, Italy, Spain and Tunisia – in West Germany, where the vaccination intake was higher, there were fewer recorded cases. This proves that if you heed the advice of the vets, who after all, have spent many years researching the subject of equine flu, you could prevent your animal suffering from or spreading the virus.

No one seems to know how or why the virus decides to strike, but once it does, because it is passed on so easily, it rushes through the equine population.

But how do you know when your horse has got flu? The answer to that one is simple – he will have a runny nose and will probably cough a lot. If flu is diagnosed by your vet, your horse must not be worked under any circumstances or you will damage his lungs. He needs veterinary care and a lot of rest until he has completely recovered.

Some people have complained in the past that when they have had their elderly horses or ponies vaccinated, some of them have been rather ill afterwards. One vet I know maintains that once the vaccination has been administered the animal must be allowed to rest for a few days to give him time to get over it. Then there should be no dramatic reaction. But, work him too soon and you could ruin him. Thousands of pounds have been spent researching this particular subject and it would be foolish to ignore the facts. To have your mount vaccinated will cost something like £8.

I must stress that the viruses 1 and 2 are contagious, and if your horse has flu it can be spread to other equines by your clothing, grooming kit or, indeed, anything with which the animal comes into contact. When he has got it, his temperature could rise to 105°F and he will be listless and very unhappy.

If you suspect your horse or pony has flu, keep him away from any other animals, keep him warm and immediately call your vet, who will prescribe the correct treatment. If you want to take your horse's temperature, insert the thermometer in his anus and hold it there for two minutes. While you are doing this, make sure you stand by the side of his rump so that if he does become frightened and kicks out, he will not hit you. The thermometer is not very big or cumbersome, and he should not object to its use. A horse's normal temperature is 100.5°F. Remember before you insert the thermometer to put some vaseline on it to make entry that much easier. Done properly, the animal will not even know that he is having his temperature taken.

I mentioned earlier that the signs of equine flu are a runny nose and a cough, among other things. I must point out that he can also develop a cough which does not lead to flu but is merely a throat irritation brought on by a change of air, or slight illness. This is nowhere near as bad as equine flu and can be treated by giving him a few smears of electuary on his tongue. You can also gently massage his throat and remember, whatever you do, do not work him.

Again, it is best to isolate him so that he does not infect others around him. If the cough is not better within a few days then you must seek veterinary advice.

One disease I get very upset about is thrush because it is generally caused by the feet being neglected or the animal standing on wet and dirty bedding for extended periods. Anyone who allows their mount to get thrush should be ashamed of themselves because, although it can be caused by things outside your control, it is often the fault of a horse or pony owner being lazy in his stable duties. This particular disease emits a foul smell and is in no way pleasant or acceptable to the horse or those connected with him.

To treat it you must first make sure that the foot is cleaned with water and that the frog (the 'V' shaped substance I explained in an earlier chapter) is free from any loose ends. When this has been done, put a large covering of stockholm tar between the cleft of the frog and then cover with a clean piece of sacking tied carefully around the foot. Make sure that you change the dressing daily until the condition has cleared up. As the frog is a living substance it must be used and will become soft, smelly and pappy if it is not. It needs the pressure of walking, so take the animal out on a lead rein so that he can not only stretch his legs but also do his feet a power of good at the same time.

If the thrush has only gained a slight hold, there is no reason why your mount should not be ridden because, again, it will provide the pressure that the frog must have to keep it healthy. The farrier can be a great help to you as far as thrush is concerned, as he knows all there is to know about feet and how to look after them.

That is one reason why you must never take the advice, or use the services of 'cowboy' farriers who have had no formal training and who could, very easily, ruin your mount for all time by destroying his feet with bad workmanship. People who keep their horses at livery normally use the same farrier as the stables and, if they have been doing so for years, you can rest easy because he will know his job. He might advise you to allow him to fit shoes which are thinner at the back than they are at the front, a design which allows the frog to come into contact with the ground more easily. It is a good idea which has worked well over the years. But since prevention is better than cure, remember to pick your horse's feet out regularly and, if he is kept in, make sure that you muck him out properly, changing his bedding when you should. This will prevent your mount getting thrush.

Now I want to deal with some all too common but easily prevented complaints – saddle sores and girth galls, which sound like a musical act but can be very uncomfortable for your mount. Saddle sores are caused by an ill-fitting saddle, or from the rider sliding about and causing friction on the horse's back, and if they appear on the withers you will have a hard time curing the damage. Even if you put a soft pad underneath the saddle to ease the pressure, the chances are it will continue to rub the injury and you will be back to square one. The only thing to do under those circumstances is not to put a saddle on the animal's back until the wound has completely healed and only then in gentle stages. Try to rush things and you will make the injury worse because it is on a part of the body that is terribly vulnerable. Only time and a lot of care can cure wither damage.

What you must do is eliminate the source of the injury and if that means replacing your saddle or learning not to sit in it like a sack of potatoes, then do so at once, otherwise the same thing will happen over and over again. Alternatively, it might be that you did not groom him properly and left some dried mud on his back, which was ground in by the saddle when you mounted. If that is the case then remember that you must always take mud off, particularly on the parts where the tack fits. If you do that, your pony or horse will not suffer unnecessarily.

Girth galls are caused by a girth being too loose, too tight or too dirty, making the skin sore when it rubs up against it. The way to cure the problem is to change the offending girth with one that is supple and clean or one which has been wrapped in lamb's wool to make it soft against the skin. If the body has been rubbed very badly then the only advice I can give you is to leave the saddle off altogether until the skin has healed. Most of these injuries can be avoided if your tack fits properly, is kept clean and the pony groomed as he should be before the tack is put on him.

Other common injuries include bruising and slight cuts or nicks around the legs which in themselves are not much but which, if they are allowed to go untreated, could cause a great deal of trouble later on through infection. Every time you return from a ride you should check that all is well with your horse by running your eyes slowly over his body, looking for any tell-tale blood flecks.

Always be sure to wash off the mud

If you find any, wash off the mud with water that has a mild disinfectant in it, in order to find out how deep the cut is and to clean away any germs. If the damage does not call for the attention of a vet, put wound powder on the cut and allow the animal to go about his normal routine. If it is deep, however, and needs stitches, then the vet must be summoned at once.

If your mount bangs one of his legs while out on a ride and when you return home you find that it has swollen, one of the best ways to bring down the swelling is to hose the bruise with cold water for several minutes. This will also ease any soreness he may be suffering. When you have finished applying the cold water treatment, dry the leg gently with a stable rubber and turn your mount out, or, if he lives in, make sure he is comfortably settled in his stable before leaving him.

* * *

The reason you should make sure the animal's legs are dried properly is that if you do not he could develop cracked heels.

Again this is a condition caused by the horse's owner's laziness. If the animal's legs were kept clean and dry, the heels would not crack and become sore. At first the skin will dry and look as though small blisters are about to break through, then small cracks will appear which will get wider and eventually cause lameless if not treated. To ease the problem clean the heels and apply zinc and castor oil ointment. As far as I am concerned, I would not ride the horse or pony until the condition is better.

When it is, put a smudge of vaseline in the heels just to give extra protection. It is really like having a slight cut in between your toes and you know how uncomfortable that can be if you do not ease the problem.

So, to prevent this sort of condition in the heels, do not forget to dry them properly when you return from a ride, particularly when it has been raining and the ground is very muddy.

Mud fever also affects the heels and the legs themselves. When a horse develops mud fever, his legs tend to swell, the skin will feel very tender and eventually scabs will break through. The cause is failure to remove the mud from the animal's skin, or washing it off and then not drying him properly. Apart from affecting the legs, it can also be prominent on the horse's tummy.

Brittle hooves can also be unpleasant for your mount so remember to keep the hooves free from mud and well oiled daily. The horn of the foot grows (that is one of the reasons why his shoes must be changed every four to six weeks) and must be kept oiled if the feet are to remain healthy. It also helps to make the animal look good and clean, which is a pointer in your favour, proving that you are doing your job as it should be done.

*   *   *

In the summer your pony might well start suffering from sweet itch, a condition which is very unpleasant and can cause the animal to rub himself raw as he tries to ease the itch which afflicts him. Apart from washing the affected parts in a dilute solution of disinfectant, you can also apply benzyl benzoate, which can be obtained from any chemist as long as you tell him what it is for. At the time of writing, I am told that Thomas Pettifer and Company Limited, of Sudbury in Suffolk, have brought out a product called 'Sweet Itch Ease' which they introduced at the BETA trade fair in February 1982. This is good news because sweet itch has been a major problem for many ponies for years. To buy the Pettifer product, ask your local tack shop owner, who will probably be able to help. If he cannot, write and ask for details straight from the manufacturers but remember to enclose a stamped, self-addressed envelope for a reply.

Sweet itch is thought, by some experts to be an allergy to midges, which are prevalent in the summer months, particularly at dawn and at dusk. So, some measure of relief can be given by stabling an affected pony from early evening until mid-morning.

Another irritating problem is concussion of the forelegs which is generally caused by working a horse or a pony on firm ground. It is also known as sore shins. If you have ever run over rugged, hard ground for any length of time, you will remember how badly your legs ached afterwards, even if you were very fit at the time. Fitness has very little to do with concussion – jarring, however, has. A lot of racehorses, or competition animals like show jumpers, suffer from it in the height of the season when there has been very little rain to ease the going. Sore shins can be extremely painful and you will probably find that if your mount is suffering from them there will be some heat emitting from the forelegs. If it is really bad they might even swell somewhat. To ease the condition you will have to hose the legs several times a day, which will reduce any swelling and make the pony feel much better.

While treatment is continuing, the animal must have complete rest and not be ridden, otherwise all your hard work will be in vain. When he is sound again, and the heat has gone out of the limbs, he may be worked gently. But, subsequently, avoid trotting on roads or any hard, uneven lanes and do not canter on anything but the softest of ground. In this way you will, one hopes, prevent a recurrence of condition.

If your pony has thin soles it is also a good idea, and in many cases, essential, to keep him away from uneven or rough, firm ground for ever. Failure to do so could lead to him bruising his feet. The farrier will tell you if your horse has thin soles because he will soon find out when shoeing him.

At some stage of your horse's life he is bound to step on something sharp, like a nail or piece of glass, which may puncture the foot and cause lameness and infection. The wound should be well cleaned after the offending object has been removed. Then apply hot kaolin poultices to relieve pain and congestion and make the pus come out. When this has been done the horse will not come to any harm and will be well on the way to recovery. Again, he must not be ridden until the wound has completely healed.

Earlier in the book, I talked about keeping the stableyard clean and tidy from foreign objects, and this is one of the reasons why. Foot damage can sometimes take ages to get better and so it is sensible to try and avoid such lameness all together. And the best way to do that is to pick up any rubbish you might see lying about the yard.

If you have a good farrier your horse or pony will not suffer from corns, provided you call him in to change your mount's shoes when you should. If you don't, and the shoes are left on the animal's feet too long, he will develop corns which, as you can imagine, can be painful. Call in the farrier and get him to pare the affected area. If an abcess has developed, the foot will have to be poulticed. When the foot is healthy again, the farrier will probably fit special shoes to make the going easier for your mount.

Another disease you may well come across is ringworm, which is highly contagious and which can strike any part of the horse's body. It will appear as small circles of bare flesh on the skin. If your horse or pony develops it, he must be isolated to stop it spreading and all his grooming kit must be disinfected. Ringworm can be caught from another animal or might even develop in yours if he is in bad condition and kept in a filthy stable.

The patchy circles will normally grow in size and scabs will form and eventually drop off. To get rid of ringworm you should paint the patches daily with tincture of iodine or go to the chemist and ask him for a tin of proper ringworm ointment. But, no matter how thorough you are, you must call in a vet to supervise the treatment because, if any of those patches are missed, other horses or ponies might catch the ringworm.

People can also catch ringworm so you must remember to protect yourself. When applying the ointment or iodine, wear an old blouse or shirt and trousers, which you or your parents can burn when you have finished the treatment. Always make sure that you wash yourself properly afterwards.

Just to play safe, because it is so highly contagious, wear rubber gloves to prevent your hands actually coming into contact with the scabs or patches. It will all take a lot of time but you must be thorough otherwise the ringworm will not be destroyed. Keep on treating the patches and spots until they are dead, which could take two or three weeks. When the infection has cleared up, all the bedding you take out of the box must be burnt and the stable washed down with disinfectant to kill any germs which may be lingering. It can be a long job, but it must be done.

12
Identification

One of the biggest problems facing today's horse and pony owners is the activities of rustlers, whose aims are to make a quick profit at the expense and misery of others. At one time they would steal in during the night when everyone was sleeping to take a horse from its stable or field. Now, they even break in during the daytime and are then on their way before the owner knows his or her horse or pony has gone missing. It is not a pleasant subject to write about, but the more you understand, the better you will be able to cope with the problem. If you are always thinking safety, then you might just foil any rustlers who may pick on you.

If your horse lives in a field, particularly if he lives in one near a main road, you must check that all is well with him every morning and evening and if your parents get the opportunity, they could also pop along during the afternoon to see that everything is all right. That way you have more chance of protecting him against thieves, and although it might seem to be a chore, I can assure you that it is necessary.

The plain fact is that up to a thousand horses, donkeys and ponies are being slaughtered every week to provide meat for overseas' markets (and this is where some stolen animals end up). They are usually bought at sales, driven to the abattoirs and put down, then shipped out in containers. Selling horses for meat is, of course, perfectly legal and many of those people who must take the blame for this thriving business are horse and pony breeders who are providing too

Watch out for rustlers

many animals for a market that is just not there. And even if it is, the animals can be bought by people who later find they cannot afford to keep them and are forced to sell. That is why so many end up in the sale ring and, if they are unlucky, being bought by a butcher or a trader in horse meat.

I hate the whole procedure and, if it were in my power to do so, I would ban the whole thing and make it impossible for horses to be sold for meat in this country. But that is only my opinion and many people disagree with me. My view of this, however, and one I stand by, is that the horse has, all through our history, given of his best for us and to treat him now merely as a food animal should be against all our basic principles. But greed or, as some might argue, necessity, is all powerful in this modern world of ours and animals, in my opinion, are getting a raw deal from it all.

While money is involved there will always be people trying to make lots of it. It really doesn't matter to them that they might have to kill horses, ponies and donkeys to achieve their aims. It does not matter if it be big business or small trade; at the end of the day it all boils down to the fact that an animal has got to die to satisfy someone's needs. That, and the principle of survival of the fittest, has been so since the beginning of time.

What I cannot tolerate are the 'cowboys' who steal to supplement their income because they are the ones who are the most dangerous. The legitimate people are those who buy hundreds of horses legally at sales. The one-off merchants, who steal a horse, pony or donkey from a field and sell it to a butcher who does not ask too many questions, are vermin and should be treated as such, for the heartache and deep sadness they cause.

That is why many people believe in freeze-branding, which is not at all painful to the animal concerned and has proved highly effective against theft. In fact, at the time of writing, more than 11,000 horses and ponies in Britain have been branded in this manner and of fourteen who have been stolen all have been successfully traced.

The company which performs freeze-branding is Farm-Key Ltd of Banbury, in Oxfordshire. If you are interested in having your mount identified, all you need to do is write to Mary Awre of FarmKey Ltd and ask for the relevant details. One of those to have taken advantage of the freeze-branding scheme is top show jumping trainer Ted Edgar, who has had some of his horses identified in this way. Many of his horses cost thousands of pounds and if they were stolen it would, indeed, be a great loss, not only in money terms but because his jumpers are well-loved and have helped make him what he is today in the world of show jumping. It is also another classic example of horses playing a major role in somebody's life.

But it is still surprising how many people would not even know how to describe their horses if they were taken, apart from, perhaps, giving the colour of the animal. The police have a tough job finding stolen horses and ponies and the task is made that much more difficult if they cannot be given a complete description of the stolen animal. The police do not ever brand their own horses, as I found when paying a visit to Imber Court, the Mounted Police Training Establishment at East Molesey, in Surrey. But they do have a graphic description of each animal in their charge which is recorded and then put on file. I might add that the police horses are beautifully kept and a credit to the mounted force.

The freeze-marking procedure does not hurt the animal in any way and because the mark is made where the saddle goes, it cannot be seen when you are riding. When applied, the super chilled marker eventually leaves a white number on the animal's skin which is clean and bold enough for everyone to see. If you are considering having it done to your mount, first ask to see a picture of a horse who has been freeze-marked so that you know exactly what it all entails.

Once the freeze-marking has been done the number given to the animal is put in a central register. FarmKey operate a twenty-four hour a day, seven days a week tracing facility which goes into action the moment they receive notification of a missing horse. They keep in constant touch with the police and give notice to slaughterhouses, sales and ports. In short, they give the villains a run for their money and it just is not advisable to go about stealing horses that have been freeze-marked. Just to show how concerned they are, the company also offers a £1,000 reward to anyone who provides information which leads to the conviction of anyone stealing a freeze-marked horse.

They are truly interested in helping the public, and their total commitment to what they believe in must be congratulated. Anything which stops the horse rustlers is a good thing.

The West Germans, on the other hand, still practise the old method of branding on the rump and, if you ever go to an international show jumping meeting, you might well see the big Hanoverian-type jumpers with a distinctive brand-mark on their quarters. I do not like this method at all, but it is not for me to question how people go about various equestrian activities abroad.

In America, in the old days, the cavalry used to mark all their mounts with branding irons so that if they were ever stolen, they would be instantly recognized as army mounts. Mind you, if you were an Apache, you probably would not care who knew anyway. The fact is, though, that all through history man has had to make his mark on things, particularly on the animals, that he has owned because there was always someone about who could take them and claim them for his own. Once a horse had been branded it was very difficult for the brand to be altered and so anyone who had intentions of stealing had to think twice before actually committing the deed.

If one goes right back in the past and studies some of the dreadful penalties for rustlers and criminals of all sorts, it is hard to envisage how on earth stealing ever flourished. If anyone stole a horse in America even just a hundred years ago he was liable to be caught by angry farmers and cowboys and promptly strung up to the nearest tree. Hard justice for hard and desperate people, but it does prove though that no matter what the deterrent there is always somebody who wants something that does not belong to him. Perhaps that is human nature. If it is that is where animals score over us every time.

If you do not want to have your horse of pony freeze-marked, or branded in any way, I can quite understand and sympathize. However, if you want to be able to help the police in the event of your horse being stolen then, as I have mentioned, you will be well advised at least to keep a detailed record of his description. To do this ask one of your parents, or a friend, to have a notebook and pencil on hand when you go to the stables so that you can read out an accurate description of the animal and have a permanent record made of it. Take in everything: colour, markings, eyes, nose, in short, anything that would help others to recognize him as yours should he be stolen. And never think that an unusual marking is too trivial to record. The more unusual a marking the easier it is to identify the animal. Also, have a photograph taken of your mount and keep the negative, so that you could have several copies reproduced if necessary to give others an idea of what he looks like.

I know of one lady whose aged horse was stolen from his

field and she spent months searching in vain for him. She circulated pictures and a description to the police and knackers' yards so that, if the animal ever turned up, there was more chance of the thief being caught. When things were really desperate she offered a very high reward for his return so much did she love and miss him. You see, it was not because he was a world beater, or even a top show animal. He was just an ordinary, old horse, who had grown to be part of this particular lady's family over the years.

She did the right thing and one day her mount was discovered in another field about twenty miles from his home, having been taken by someone who wanted a horse but could not afford to buy one. The police caught the culprit and the old gelding was safely returned to his grateful owner. The whole episode proved to me that love and affection is far greater than any money. When the woman concerned offered that reward, it represented a substantial part of her savings yet she was prepared to give it away without a second thought to have the horse she loved back in the safety of her ownership. That, to me, is what life, and being a horse owner, is really all about.

13
A job with horses

I would like to have a shiny new ten pence piece for every time I have heard a youngster say, 'When I leave school I am going to work with horses.' The majority never will, for a multitude of reasons, though I do have to concede that it is a romantic notion and one which for some may well become reality. But I would not be honest with you if I did not tell you now that there are some unscrupulous people in the horse world who will attempt to exploit you and get away with paying you slave-like wages, and only giving you one day off every two or three weeks. Things became so bad at once stage that union leaders complained bitterly and many worried parents wrote to newspapers and magazines asking for help in order to expose those who were being unfair to their children. One only has to look back through history to discover that working with horses as a groom or stableboy was considered by many uninformed people as only one step above being a roadsweeper. The fact that some youngsters were entrusted with expensive racehorses or prized hunters did not seem to matter. As far as some bosses were concerned, you did your job, in all weathers, did not have an opinion and jumped when you were told to for a pittance of a wage.

Improvements, particularly in the racing world, have been made and there are now definite guide-lines about basic wages and hours of work. It took years of negotiation between union representatives and trainers but I think both sides would agree that the situation is better now that is has ever been. Nowadays both boys and girls work in racing stables and both can become professional riders. But, unless you are utterly dedicated, the chances of you surviving an apprenticeship and actually riding in public is remote. I know that to be a fact, having spent seven years in a National Hunt stable and having held a professional jockey's licence for three of those years. During that time many talented people became disheartened with the lack of opportunities and, although they loved horses and riding, left the industry altogether. That, in fact, is one of the great shames about racing – there is so much waste.

If you read this and still want to be a jockey, or jockette, the first thing you must do while you are still at school is write to the trainer you would like to work for and ask if you could be considered for a trial during the school holidays. If he is looking for staff you might be in luck, particularly if you have already learned to ride ponies. The style, of course, is totally different, but if you know how to sit on a horse properly you will have some chance of reaching the interview stage. You might even be lucky enough to be sent to the 'Jockey School' which, at the time of writing, is run by former ace jockey Johnny Gilbert at Goodwood. Many boys have left his care and gone on to be very good riders themselves. He knows exactly what is required and passes his expert knowledge on to the youngsters. The scheme, which is funded by the Horserace Betting Levy Board, takes about six boys and four girls from the age of 16, who are taught to ride properly and to do stable work. The course lasts for six weeks.

Remember, however, that to be a jockey on the Flat you must be very light and at 15 should not weigh much more than six stone. For National Hunt racing, where the horses carry bigger weights, you can afford to be about eight stone on leaving school. Being tall does not matter and, on occasions, can prove beneficial, because a good length of leg will serve you in good stead when riding over fences and hurdles.

If after an apprenticeship you do not make the grade as a jockey, there are several other jobs in racing which may

What do you mean, you want to practise on me!

appeal to you. You can care for the racehorses as a lad with prospects of promotion to head lad or travelling head lad (taking the horses to the race courses).

For those who do not want to ride, but would like to work amongst horses and have had secretarial training, a job as secretary to a racehorse trainer can be very rewarding.

Not everyone wants to ride horses. Many youngsters in this country would dearly love to become blacksmiths, nowadays a very rewarding and vital position in the horse world. I remember one blacksmith telling me how much he was respected and that he was doing so well he could afford to take on two apprentices and have a holiday abroad each year. That was good news because he worked very hard, was good at his job and most certainly gave value for money. To become a blacksmith you need to serve an apprenticeship with a master farrier and, apart from working in the forge, will also be required to spend a lot of your time at college studying for exams. It is not as easy as many people think and the rewards early on are not very high. But if you persevere, work hard and digest the knowledge which is imparted, when you do become qualified you will probably never be out of work. For further information you could write to the Worshipful Company of Farriers, enclosing a self-addressed, stamped envelope, and ask them for some details. The address is 3 Hamilton Road, Cockfosters, Barnet, Herts EN4 9EU.

If you just want to work with horses as a groom, then the best thing you can do is work at a local stable in your spare time and school holidays and learn all you can about grooming, mucking out, feeding and riding. If you are really keen you could train at a school for the Association of British Riding School's Groom's Diploma, a really worthwhile qualification for anyone wishing to earn a living caring for horses or ponies. Helping out at your local riding school does not really qualify you to care for horses such as show jumpers, eventers or hunters. Obtaining this Diploma will ensure that you can demand realistic wages as you are trained for the job. When you are qualified you can go on and ask for a job anywhere in the show jumping, hunting or eventing world or in a livery yard. I would like to advise you on a couple of points. When you are at an interview (and always take a parent along with you) and you like what you are being told about a possible job, politely insist that rates of pay and time off are put in writing.

If you intend to work away from home, and accommodation is being offered, it is always a good idea to go along and inspect it. What might sound like a paradise could easily be, or turn into, a hell on earth. So, have a look, and satisfy yourself that all is well. Once you have done this, you will feel much happier and so will your parents. They cannot be with you all the time and the sooner you start making constructive decisions for yourself, the better. Before you go to any interview, write down all the questions you can think of and memorize them. That way you should not meet with any unforeseen problems.

If you want to work for a show jumper or event rider, find

Check accommodation before you take the job

out their address by writing to the British Show Jumping Association or the British Horse Society, both of whom reside at Stoneleigh in Warwickshire. Do not run away with the idea though that you will become a famous rider. That takes talent, dedication and a great deal of money and if you cannot find enough sponsorship, or, indeed, any at all, your chances of even starting are remote. It sometimes happens that a rider will, after a while, allow you to compete on some of his or her horses – but that is fairly rare. Competition horses are very expensive and if anything goes wrong a rider could lose his livelihood.

Some people are not interested in competition riding, but like to devote their time to teaching others to ride. To do that officially, however, you will need to pass exams to become, initially, a British Horse Society Assistant Instructor/Instructress (AI) which qualifies you to teach under supervision. After further exams and a lot of hard work you might be good enough to qualify for your BHSII which means you are then an Intermediate Instructor.

Then, to become fully qualified, you must pass the British Horse Society Instructor's examination. The highest award is that of Fellow of the British Horse Society but very few achieve it. If you are interested in becoming an instructor you should write for advice to the British Horse Society, whose address is The British Equestrian Centre, Stoneleigh, Warwickshire. Again, enclose a self-addressed, stamped envelope. They will give you further details of approved training centres and examination syllabi.

Even if you are bright enough to pass all the examinations, it still does not mean that you will automatically go out and earn vast sums of money. You will need, first, to find a suitable job for your talents and to do that may mean travelling and leaving home. Once you are qualified, however, money can be earned to supplement your income by teaching youngsters in your spare time or setting up a riding clinic of your own. But you need to be living in the right area, where there are plenty of horses and fairly well-off owners.

One of the advantages of being an instructor is that you

can go out and teach people at their own stables, which means that you do not have the expense of running your own. This cuts down on bills and the more people you teach the better known you become. I know of one event rider who makes a very good living showing people the best way to prepare themselves for horse trials. He is, however, a competitor of international standing, who has ridden for Britain and so knows what he is talking about. He gained his knowledge and experience by riding all over the world.

Some people's talents lie not in riding but in looking after horses and ponies in their spare time and helping out with disabled riders. This, really, is the best of both worlds because not only are you close to the animals you love, but you are doing a worthwhile voluntary job as well. But I must stress that it is voluntary and you cannot expect to get paid for being a helper. What does a helper do? Normally they help to groom the ponies, put their saddles and bridles on and then, with another person who is helping out, walk alongside a handicapped child when he or she is riding. Although there is no money in it for you, what you will discover is that it is most rewarding in other ways. Anyone who has seen the sheer delight on a handicapped child's face as he leaves the wheelchair and is helped into the saddle, will know what I mean. If you want to help out all you have to do is write to the Riding For The Disabled Organization, whose base, again, is at Stoneleigh, or ask at your local riding school who runs a riding for the disabled group in your area.

There are also people, highly experienced equestrians, who travel horses abroad. Certainly it is a job which helps you to see the world but, at times, it can also be quite dangerous, particularly if a horse becomes frightened while flying from one country to another. There is always a vet on board the aircraft, as well, but someone who is travelling horses by air has got to have a wealth of experience and know exactly what they are doing at all times. It is a position which is best thought about once you have spent several years working with horses.

Another area of working with horses I would like to touch upon is that connected with the rest homes in Britain. They employ staff to look after the animals and, I might add, do a wonderful job. If it was not for organizations like the Bransby Home of Rest for Horses and the Ada Cole Memorial Homes and others, many horses and ponies would not survive. The homes provide shelter, food and care for them when they have probably given up hope of ever being looked after properly again.

As you can imagine, with the amount of work they have to do, the homes are labour-intensive and the qualification you need more than anything is a caring attitude. Some of the animals have gone through a wretched time and barely trust anyone. Slowly but surely the people at the rest homes make them well again, both mentally and physically, so that in time they begin to think life is worth living after all.

Some young people have definite ideas about what breed of horses they want to work with and another worthwhile area to think about is the breeding industry, Thoroughbreds in particular. I say 'in particular' because research has shown me that too many horses and ponies have been bred in the past when the demand for them was almost non-existent. As I mentioned earlier, too many end up being sent to the sales where they are usually mishandled, abused and sometimes bought as meat for the foreign trade.

At least Thoroughbred breeding for racing is productive and, indeed, a very big industry nowadays. One only has to look at places like Ireland and America, who deal in millions of pounds when buying and selling horses, to realize just how big the whole business is. Working at a stud can also be highly rewarding for you, too, not so much perhaps in the monetary sense but in being happy in your work. You are, as it were, in at the beginning from the time that the mare is introduced to the stallion to the day that the foal is born and eventually old enough to be weaned from its mother. It is, I know, a fascinating experience bringing a new animal into the world, particularly one which might, just might, grow up to be one of the fastest equines on four legs. Apart from helping the stud groom, your duties would also include the usual stable chores, but to a much higher degree. Studs are kept spotlessly clean because of the fear of infection and, therefore, anyone who works at one can expect to be working hard most of the time. It is most certainly not a job for somebody who is looking for an easy time.

There are studs all over the country but, as Newmarket is deemed to be the home of racing, some of the best in the world, including the National Stud, are based there. Apart from racehorses there are many other breeding establishments who deal in Arabs, Welsh ponies, Cobs, Exmoors, Connemaras and so on. And for those of you who are interested, here are some useful addresses:

The Highland Pony Society, Rowan Cottage, Balendoch, Meigle, Perthshire.
The New Forest Pony Society, Beacon Corner, Burley, Ringwood, Hampshire
The Shetland Pony Stud Book Society, Montrose, Angus, Scotland
Connemara Pony Breeders Society, Ard-na-Mara, Salthill, Galway, Ireland
The English Connemara Pony Society, Buttermilk Farm, Leafield, Oxfordshire
The Norwegian Fjord Breed Society, Maple Stud, Ewhurst, Cranleigh, Surrey
The National Pony Society, 7 Cross-and-Pillory Lane, Alton, Hampshire

If you write to any of these establishments, please enclose a stamped, self-addressed envelope for a reply.

If you are really keen on a career as a stud hand you can train for the National Pony Society's Stud Assistant's Certificate and Diploma. Write to the Society for details of the examinations and a list of studs which take on students.

If you want to travel as well as to support the horse cause and maybe do some welfare work in your own time on a voluntary basis, there are several organizations abroad, apart from ones in Britain, who might welcome your help. The major one in Egypt for instance, is the Brooke Hospital for Animals in Cairo. They can be contacted in England at British Columbia House, 1 Regent Street, London W1.

Another such organization is the Greek Animal Welfare Fund, 4–6 Whyteleafe Road, Purley, Surrey.

If you just want to be near horses when you go on holiday, you would do well to know the address of the English Riding Holidays and Trekking Association, because they have a comprehensive list of riding schools. They reside at Homestead Farm, Charlton Musgrave, Wincanton, Somerset. The schools on the list they send you are of a very high standard and are used to dealing with all sorts of riders, from beginners to the more experienced.

If you would like to know more about donkeys there are several very good publications that would interest you: *Donkey Wrinkles and Tales* by Marjorie Dunkels, and *Training Your Donkey* by the same authoress; *Donkeys, their Care and Management* by P. R. De Wesselow; and *Keeping A Donkey* by Dorothy Morris. These are all available from the Donkey Breed Society Trading Officer. The address is Manor Farm Cottage, Buckland, Broadway, Worcestershire, WR12 7LY. Write to the Trading Officer, Michael Northern, to find out what it costs to become a member of the Donkey Breed Society. There is junior and senior membership and the Society is affiliated to the British Horse Society.

I include donkeys in this chapter because they are as important as horses and ponies and are used for a multitude of pastimes, apart from giving children rides along the beach. They also give a great deal of pleasure to many thousands of people and their interests must be held in the highest regard.

If you want to know anything about them, or are interested in working with them, I am sure the Donkey Breed Society would be only too pleased to help. You see, they care as well, and that is vitally important where animals are concerned. I live for the day when ignorance about horses, ponies and donkeys and, of course, other animals is wiped out. That is one of my reasons for writing this book. If you want to work among them I wish you the best of luck. I know that you will probably enjoy every moment as long as you do not expect to earn a fortune – the money, rightly, is spent on those in your care.

Index